Literary Wal

HERTFORDSHIRE

Literary Walks In
HERTFORDSHIRE

Alex Reeve

HiP
HISTORY INTO PRINT

First published by
History into Print, 56 Alcester Road,
Studley, Warwickshire B80 7LG in 2007
www.history-into-print.com

ISBN 10: 1 85858 316 0
ISBN 13: 978 1 85858 316 7

The moral right of the author has been asserted.

A Cataloguing in Publication Record
for this title is available from the British Library.

Typeset in Times
Printed in Great Britain by
SupaPrint (Redditch) Limited
www.supaprint.com

CONTENTS

FOREWORD

A bout five or six years ago I walked into a bookshop in Welwyn Garden City and asked a young lady serving at the counter if she had a book of walks about the writers of Hertfordshire and their literary works. She told me that such a book didn't exist, then she said, "Why don't you write one - it would fly off the shelves?" I smiled and left the shop but the thought stayed with me. "Why not?" I asked myself.

So I bought some maps of Hertfordshire, read biographies of the authors and some of their works and marched around the county. The work was truly a labour of love. The writers lived in diverse and delightful locations, which for aesthetic reasons alone are well worth visiting. The locations have also influenced their work and to discover passages that precisely mirror corners of our county has been very rewarding.

Each chapter comprises a short biography of the writer, directions to his town or village, a diagram of the route of the walk with detailed instructions to assist you on your way around, and an occasional quote.

I have tried to be accurate with all details and information. I hope you find the route easy enough to follow. Above all I hope you enjoy your walk.

Walk 1:

SIR FRANCIS BACON: VISCOUNT OF

ST ALBANS, RESIDENT OF GORHAMBURY: 6 MILES

INTRODUCTION

The undisputed achievements of Sir Francis Bacon would represent an outstanding career for very many of us. If the more contentious accomplishments that have been attributed to him are true, then he must rank as one of the most extraordinary and most talented individuals ever to have lived in England.

That being so, and given that England has a modern service economy in which businesses connected to leisure and tourism thrive, it is surprising that St Albans has not promoted the connection with their home grown genius to greater effect. Towns and cities across the realm make good use of the heritage that chance has bequeathed them. St Albans does too: there are museums, galleries and a wide range of cultural activities available to residents and visitors. Few of these relate to Bacon.

Half-a-million visitors flock to Stratford-Upon-Avon each year to visit the birthplace of a shrewd Tudor merchant and businessman; and a brilliant playwright. The visitors are seeing the town where William Shakespeare was born and where he went to school (although there is no record of his ever having attended). They visit the house of his wife and that of his illiterate daughter. They go to the theatre to see a Shakespeare play and to enjoy a rich cultural experience.

Consider then that there are many scholars, familiar with the evidence of the authorship of Shakespeare's plays, who believe that the man who lived in

Stratford did not write them. The scholars are divided but many believe that the man who lived in St Albans, Sir Francis Bacon, might have and almost certainly was involved with them. Yet visit the tourist office and politely ask for information about Bacon and the staff will point you in the direction of the private estate at Gorhambury. Ask about our man and the town and you will draw a blank. Ask down at the museum that borders his estate and you will draw a second blank. But the signs of Bacon's connection with the town are there - maybe not in abundance - but in sufficient quantity to provide you with an interesting and illuminating walk.

AN ORTHODOX BIOGRAPHY OF SIR FRANCIS BACON

Queen Elizabeth I was a frequent visitor to Gorhambury. On one occasion she asked a young Francis Bacon his age; she was probably delighted with his courtly reply, "Just two years younger than Your Majesty's happy reign." The Queen referred to him as her "young Lord Keeper" for his father Sir Nicholas Bacon was the Lord Keeper of the Great Seal, a high office at the Tudor Court. Francis Bacon's mother was Lady Anne Cooke, a puritan scholar, fluent in Latin, French and Italian, and very capable in Greek.

Francis was born on 22 January 1561 in York House on the Strand in London and brought up at Gorhambury. Sir Nicholas and Lady Anne took the education of Francis seriously and he was tutored at St Albans School and at home in arithmetic, geometry, astronomy, the arts of music and rhetoric, European languages and literature, history, ancient learning, Greek and Bible studies. Francis was an exceptionally talented student; he impressed his tutors and at the age of twelve, his parents deemed him ready for University and sent him to Trinity College, Cambridge. It seems, however, that Cambridge wasn't ready for him: Francis was disappointed by his experience there and thought that the professors had little to contribute.

The contrast between the enriching home education and the inadequate offering of Cambridge touched him deeply. In time it would drive him to dedicate his life to the advancement of scholarship and civilisation. But that would come later; for now he had to pursue a career and he entered Gray's Inn to study law.

In 1577, Francis joined the suite of Elizabeth's Ambassador to France and remained there for three years until the death of his father prompted his return to England. His father's death was a significant event: at eighteen he was the youngest son and seemingly the most unfortunate too, being the one child of four to have been overlooked in his father's will. Sir Nicholas's legacy to him comprised a name and an education, but no money. Being penniless, Francis was faced with the tricky task of earning a living; being shrewd, he solicited the aid of his relatives: the highly influential Cecil family.

They did not encourage him. When he was older, and probably in reflective mood, he wrote an essay entitled Of Great Place which was published in his book The Advancement of Learning. The essay touches on sycophancy and the pursuit of power: it reveals the unpleasantness of the task that was occupying Bacon. The passage below conveys a poignancy still relevant to the ambitious man or woman in the 21st Century:

"It is a strange desire, to seek power and lose liberty, or to seek power over others and to lose power over a man's self. The rising unto place is laborious, and by indignities men come to dignities. The standing is slippery, and the regress is either a downfall or at least an eclipse: which is a melancholy thing."

Francis eventually earned his living as a barrister and in 1584, he entered Parliament as MP for Melcombe, the first of several constituencies that he represented. His genius emerged and in time he became the leading parliamentarian of his age. He was also brave: in a house full of lawyers he proposed a widespread reform of the law, arguing that the law should exist to guard the rights of the people - not to feed lawyers. This was too strong for the House of Commons. His Outline of Law Review was published and ignored in England. It was translated into French and studied across the Channel; The Review became the basis for the French Civil Code, the Code Napoleon - in large part the basis of European Law today.

In Tudor England, the wool trade became highly profitable. Sheep require grass: arable land was given over to pasture, common land was enclosed, the grazing rights of ordinary people were taken away and ploughmen were left unemployed. Bacon championed the ploughmen in Parliament: he proposed that all land turned to pasture since the Queen's accession should be restored to the yeoman and the plough. The Commons passed his Bill; the Peers received it in amazement and the monarch was distinctly unimpressed. They sent the bill back with a large number of amendments. The Commons, headed by Bacon, met with the Lords, headed by Sir Edward Coke, with a view to compromise. Bacon won the day and the Bill, largely intact, passed onto the Statute Book (39 Elizabeth 1 and 2).

Unsurprisingly, Bacon was highly regarded in the country but fell out of favour at Court. He continued to speak on behalf of the common man on the important social issues of the day, e.g. Abuses in the Taverns, The Sale of Crown Offices and Lands, as well as on matters of state e.g. The Bill of Union with Scotland. But his real zeal was for study and he undertook to fill his mind with all aspects of human learning, ancient and modern. He approached his subjects logically and was dismissive of ill-thought through or incoherent doctrines. He laid the foundations to a broad based scientific order that had the purpose of raising humanity to a state of rational enlightenment. "I have taken all knowledge to be my province." He wrote in a letter to Lord Burghley.

On the accession of James I, being a favourite of the King, Bacon's fortunes changed. He was promoted in turn to the office of Attorney General, Lord Keeper, Lord Chamberlain and then ennobled first as Baron Verulam then as Viscount St Alban. Then he fell. He was accused of accepting bribes as Lord Chancellor, a practice common amongst men of his rank. He pleaded guilty, was banished from Court, fined and despatched to the Tower.

Bacon did not stay in the Tower for long and on his release found he was no longer welcome at Court, so he retreated to his estate at Gorhambury and dedicated himself to his great project: that of the education of his countrymen.

In our current age there is a vast array of books, magazines and newspapers available to the public. In the sixteenth century, the language of culture was Latin; Gower, Chaucer and very few others had written in English. The majority of the population could not read, indeed there was effectively nothing for them to read. The people who lived in this age had very limited opportunities to express or develop ideas. They were hindered through the lack of a language and education that would enable them to work through ideas. J.P. Baxter discusses the issue in The Greatest of Literary Problems:

The masses were unable to read.....London with a population of hardly two hundred thousand, reeked with filth and disease as faulty in sanitary conditions as the worse Oriental city of today. Carrion kites served to clean the streets, floors were covered with rushes to hide the dirt. Its

Sir Francis Bacon's house at Gorhambury.

inhabitants were so vicious and degraded that they flocked to witness the
brutal executions which were of daily occurrence, railing and jeering at
the victims, and finding their delight in sports too cruel for description.

Bacon thought that education could counter the depravity of the populace
and he called his project to encourage learning The Great Instauration. He
believed that a nation that was truly great would have the greatest number of
contented men and women enjoying a mental and spiritual quality dependent on
education and ethics. His ideas of the greatness of a country differed from that
of many of his peers, many of whom could not see beyond a system of privileged classes ruling illiterate lower orders, coarsened by poverty and vulgarity.

The Great Instauration was divided into six parts of which only three were
finished. The first was The Advancement of Learning, which is a series of philosophical and practical essays. The second part, Novum Organum, held to be his
greatest work, categorizes learning into a range of disciplines and reasons that,
before a statement is accepted as true, it should be supported by direct observa-

tion or experiment: a reasoning accepted as orthodox scientific methodology today. The third and last of the completed project was a philosophical treatise, The New Atlantis, which describes life among a Utopian community on a South Sea Island, resonant of Sir Thomas More's work 100 years earlier.

Bacon led a full life and his death came in his 61st year. It came bizarrely as a result of an infection caught when out in a snowstorm experimenting with the preservation of a chicken by filling it with snow. He was a talented man who gave much to the people of his and subsequent generations, whichever biography you believe to be true.

BRIEF NOTES ON THE MORE CONTENTIOUS BIOGRAPHY OF BACON

Though disputed and unproved, many scholars believe that Bacon led a group of 46 writers and translators to write the King James version of the Bible. As indicated earlier there is also the more hotly disputed notion that Bacon wrote the Shakespeare plays. There is much frenzied discussion on both these subjects, which can be seen by entering Bacon and Shakespeare on your preferred computer search engine and studying the results or reading John Mitchell's detective approach to the subject in Who Wrote Shakespeare? The evidence that the writer finds most intriguing is the design of the opening letter of The Tempest in the 1623 First Folio Edition of the Shakespeare plays. The B of Boteswaine is surrounded by irregular scrolls. A closer inspection reveals the scrolls to be the letters that comprise the name Francis Bacon. "Not proof," you may say, but nevertheless interesting. To satisfy the sceptic it should be said that there are other scrolls around the B in addition to those shown; it should also be said that this was an age of ciphers and masques where secrecy was a delight. The discovery was published by the Cincinnati Times-Star newspaper in 1931 and by The Literary Digest. The article is reproduced opposite for you to inspect:

6

LOCATION OF THE WALK AND ACCESS:

By train: St Albans is served by Thameslink and trains run frequently to the city from Bedford, Luton, Kings Cross and East Croydon.

By car: from J8 on the M1, take the A414 then follow signs for St Albans on the A4147 and A5183 to the city centre.

The walk starts at the tourist office in the market square, St Albans, which is in Chequer Street opposite the junction of Victoria Street. There are several car parks nearby and the railway station is a brisk ten minute walk away. As you leave the station turn right and right again into Victoria Street; Chequer Street and the tourist office are at the top of the hill.

THE WALK

Stand with your back to the tourist office: turn right and right again along the main road, i.e. into Chequer Street. At the traffic lights continue down into Holywell Hill. In the middle ages this street was lined with inns to accommo-date the pilgrims and other travellers who sought lodgings within the city. Many of these timber framed buildings, some with a later Georgian brick façade, have survived and one is the White Hart. Pop into the shop next door at number 23, called Pots of Art - once part of the White Hart - and ask to view (or peer in through the window) the 16th century wall painting of a hunt scene from Shakespeare's poem Venus and Adonis, where the hero is gored to death by a boar (the scene is reproduced below). The painting has been described by Dr Clive Rouse, a mural expert, as "a major national treasure" and the "finest Elizabethan wall painting outside the great houses like Hampton Court." The hunt scene from Venus and Adonis as depicted in the wall mural in Pots of Art:

But this foul grim and urchin-snouted boar,
Whose downward eye still looketh for a grave,
Ne'er saw the beauteous livery that he wore:
Witness the entertainment that he gave.
If he did see his face, why then I know
He thought to kiss him, and hath killed him so.

'Tis true, 'tis true; thus was Adonis slain;
He ran upon the boar with his sharp spear
Who did not whet his teeth at him again
But by a kiss thought to persuade him there,
And, nuzzling in his flank, the loving swine
Sheathed unaware the tusk in his soft groin.

Part of the 16th C. Wall painting of the hunt scene from Venus and Adonis
in Pots of Art Holywell Hill.

'Had I been toothed like him, I must confess
With kissing him I should have killed him first;
But he is dead, and never more did he bless
My youth with his, the more I am accursed.'
With this she falleth in the place she stood,
And stains her face with his congealed blood.

In the 16th century the White Hart was the nearest inn to Bacon's home in Gorhambury and it is thought that Bacon, a Freemason, held lodge meetings here. Bacon's crest is a boar's head - similar to that in the painting (hidden behind the wooden frame to the right of the picture). Look closely above the boar's head and you may make out a house which shares many features with Bacon's house at Gorhambury: next to the house is a hill (quite difficult to see as it's high up and behind the frame), thought to be the mound in Prae Wood where Bacon viewed the night sky through a telescope. Could it have been commissioned by Sir Francis? It is difficult to tell as the boar is not spoken of kindly in Venus and Adonis, but it does seem likely that Bacon was involved in some way. There is another smaller wall mural in The White Hart pub, on the panelled staircase which you may also like to inspect.

When you leave cross the road to the Abbey. Enter through the west tower and you approach the shrine of St Alban via the longest nave in the country. In the 16th Century, there was a wall just beyond the shrine, then a metre or two further on there was a second wall. There was a path in the space between the walls that schoolboys trudged along on their way to lessons which took place in the Lady Chapel. The stonework in the Lady Chapel up to about head height is Victorian; above that it is 13th Century. Look at the upper stone work: there are many damaged carvings. There are two theories to explain the damage: one is that it is the result of the dissolution of the monasteries. A second and more intriguing theory is that the damage was caused by unruly 15th and 16th century schoolboys, God bless 'em, of whom Francis Bacon was one. So the Lady Chapel housed St Albans School and the rascally Francis walked here from Gorhambury for his lessons. On a more sober note his father, Sir Nicholas, provided assistance for the school in the form of a Wine Charter, which helped to ensure its prosperity for 300 years. In 1871 the school relocated to its current site at the Abbey Gateway; built in 1362 and all that remains of the medieval monastery.

The Lady Chapel, St Albans. [Reproduced with kind permission of St Albans Abbey]

Leave the Abbey via the West Tower, turn right into Abbey Mill Lane then left into Fishpool street. Walk down the elegant street to the Blue Anchor and turn left into St Michael's Street, over the bridge that spans the river Ver. St Michael's, the parish church of Gorhambury (which used to be a much larger village) is further along on the left. Enter the church: in the chantry there is a statue of Sir Francis Bacon in white marble. His posture is interesting: he is seated with his right hand broken and resting over the chair: a gesture which symbolises the giving of one's life for others. The left hand supports the head, but is hidden: symbolising cryptic thought; he wears a hat: befitting a man of high rank; his eyes are open and he is gazing above the altar: gestures thought to symbolise the understanding of mysteries. Whoever commissioned the statue undoubtedly thought highly of the deceased. That man was Sir Thomas Meautys,

Bacon's private secretary, who was rewarded for his work by the bequest of the Gorhambury estate on Bacon's death. Sir Thomas married Anne Bacon, the niece of Sir Francis and his tombstone is on the floor in front of the chancel rail.

The Latin epitaph, when translated, reads:

Francis Bacon
Baron of Verulam, Viscount St Albans
or, by more conspicuous titles,
of science the light, of eloquence the law,
sat thus.

Who after all natural wisdom
and secrets of civil life he had unfolded
nature's law fulfilled -
Let compounds be dissolved. In the year of our Lord 1626, aged 66.

Of such a man, that the memory
might remain,
Thomas Meautys
living his attendant, dead his admirer,
places this monument.

When you leave the church, turn left. When you come to the main road cross over and go along Gorhambury Drive which leads alongside the Roman amphitheatre, (and is well worth a visit.) If you even half accept the hotly disputed idea that Bacon wrote the Shakespeare plays, then it is interesting to speculate whether any were ever put on here. Carry on along the drive with the River Ver flowing a short distance away. About 600 yards further along the Hollows Ditch harbouring the Roman wall will cross the path and soon after the path will veer to the left and lead up to the neo-Palladian house built in 1777. It is a fine house but our chief interest lies in the ruins of the Tudor house a little further on.

Your approach is alongside the East wing of Gorhambury. In Bacon's time there was an outer entrance beyond a courtyard that would extend into the field in front of the house today. The main entrance is the one that you can see; the servants' quarters were on the right as you entered - the lower floor nearest the road housed the cellar and the butler's pantry. On the left were quarters for the Bacon family and their guests, there was also a long gallery on the upper floor, which had stained glass windows: happily these have been preserved and re-used in the construction of the new Gorhambury house. There was a chapel in which the altar unusually was under the West window (and would have been about where the horse chestnut tree is now). Under the long gallery there were cloisters and a gilt statue of Henry VIII stood near the mound by the horse chestnut tree. The mound covers the ruins of an underground chamber where it is thought Masonic rituals took place. The forest that you can in the far distance, is Prae Wood and the hill in the centre is the site where Bacon carried out his astronomical observations (and is the hill depicted in the wall mural seen earlier).

Bacon seems to have been aware of the inadequacy of scientific knowledge of his age but satisfied himself with the idea that experiments were taking place. In the Advancement of Learning he writes of the experimentation that surrounded alchemy in these terms:

"It may be compared to the husbandman whereof Aesop makes the fable; that, when he died, told his sons that he had left unto them gold buried under ground in his vineyard; and they digged over all the ground, and gold they found none; but by reason of their stirring and digging the mould about the roots of their vines, they had a great vintage the year following: so assuredly the search and stir to make gold hath brought to light a great number of good and fruitful inventions and experiments, as well for the disclosing of nature as for the use of man's life."

When you have finished examining the ruins continue along the path. It will turn left and right several times and eventually you will leave the Gorhambury estate and go under a road bridge.

Stay with the path until you reach the main road. Turn left and walk along the main road for a while, under the motorway (M10) and cross over when you can. Take the footpath when you reach it about four hundred metres beyond the motorway bridge on the right. The path leads up a mild slope and alongside a field. When you come to the corner of the field, turn left through the rather overgrown wood, and when you emerge the other side, turn right. Now walk along to the corner of the field, which should now be on your left. Turn left at the corner alongside a hedge. At the far end of the hedge, if the weather

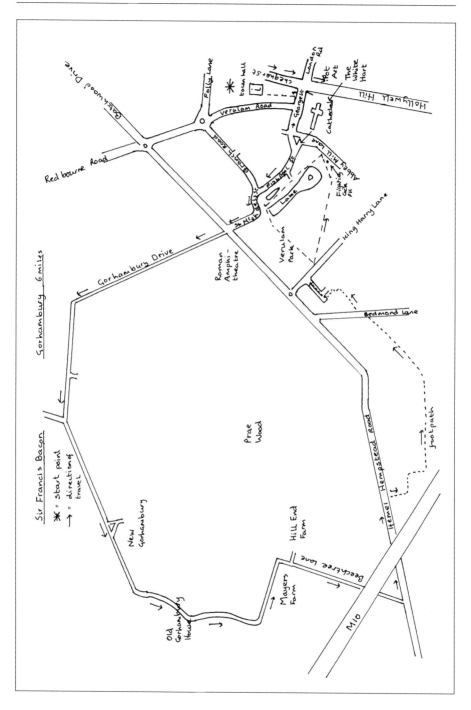

is clear, you might be able to see the Abbey in the distance. A line of oak trees points the way: beat a path across the open field towards the abbey using the oak trees as your guide. When you leave the last oak tree behind you, veer slightly to the left towards a gap in the hedge in the copse on the horizon. There is a post in the middle of the field to guide you.

Turn left beyond the hedge onto a quiet country road (Bedmond Lane) and then right a few metres further on when you see another footpath sign. The path takes you through some land that has been left unused and is now turning to scrub. The path leads to a road, but turn left onto another path Just before the road and follow it as it turns left and right before emerging adjacent to a new housing estate. The pollarded trees that border the path are testament to the fact that this land was once part of well used ancient woodland. Walk by the two parallel lines of newly planted trees that border the development to a gate that leads onto a main road. Turn right, cross over by the pedestrian traffic lights and continue straight onto the path through the gap in the hedge on the other side of the road.

A marvellous view of the Abbey will soon open up before you. Make for the greyish white building at the bottom of the hill, then for the tennis courts. Carry straight on to the left of the courts and cross the bridge that straddles the lake. Turn right on the far side and walk to the end of the lake and turn left. The path will lead alongside "Ye Olde Fighting Cocks," reputedly the oldest pub in the country. March up the hill to the Great Gateway of the Monastery. Keep to the right after the gate and then turn right into George Street, which leads uphill to the High Street. Turn right and cross over at the pedestrian traffic lights by the Clock Tower; follow the path either side of the Tower which will lead you to the market square and the beginning of the walk.

BIBLIOGRAPHY AND FURTHER READING:

Baxter, J.P. The Greatest of Literary Problems. 1915. Reprint: New York: AMS Press, 1971.

Bacon, Francis. The Promus. 1594-1596.

Bacon, Francis. The Advancement of Learning. 1605.

Bacon, Francis. Novum Organum. 1620.

Bacon, Francis. The New Atlantis. 1627.

Bacon, Francis. Essays.

Shakespeare, William. Venus and Adonis. 1623.

Walk 2:

E. M. FORSTER AND ROOK'S NEST: 6 MILES

E. M. FORSTER

Rarely can a writer's individual style be so distinctly attributable to early childhood influence as is the case with E. M. Forster. He wrote with delicacy and revealed an insight and understanding of the female persona that few male writers have attained. It therefore comes as no surprise to learn that his father died while he was very young and he was brought up by his mother and an array of adoring female relatives. He was effectively his mother's only child (she had another who died soon after birth) and he lived with his mother, with occasional separations, until her death in 1945.

Forster was born on New Year's Day in 1879. His father died soon after from consumption. The family blamed Lily, Forster's mother for not spotting the signs, and Lily blamed herself. Lily and Morgan, mother and child, then lived a gypsy-like existence, staying with a succession of friends for short periods. In the autumn of 1882, they finally settled into a large isolated house in Stevenage, set in four acres of farmland called Rook's Nest. Lily was concerned about its location but Morgan loved it, and his affection for the house shines out from the pages of Howard's End, his fourth novel.

Given the loss of her husband and child, Lily was understandably anxious about her son's health and mollycoddled him. She was, however, aware that Forster's life was a sheltered one and she encouraged visits by neighbouring boys of a similar age, who when they played with him were exasperated by his girlish ways. Although more robust than his mother believed, Forster was slight of frame and very much an intellectual. At school he felt lonely and iso-

Rook's Nest or Howard's End.

lated; as he entered his teenage years his developing homosexuality became more defined: his peers sensed it and bullied him. He did not enjoy school.

Forster went on to study at Cambridge, a place where being slight of frame, an intellectual and a homosexual were no longer drawbacks, and he blossomed. He was a member of The Apostles - an elite secret society - and The Bloomsbury Group. He graduated with a degree in classics and history.

In 1905 Forster's first novel, Where Angels Fear to Tread was published to wide acclaim. The Longest Journey followed and in 1908 he wrote A Room With A View in which he described a woman's love of a man with great poignancy and rare skill. The book is rated by some as one of the finest novels of the twentieth century though Forster himself considered Howard's End to be his best work. The latter is set in a town called Hilton which Forster modelled on Stevenage. It introduced the Wilcox, the

Schlegel and the Bast families to the Edwardians. The story unfolds with a gentle grace - the narrative and dialogue are interlaced with an exquisite commentary displaying deep emotional insight. Hitherto, Forster had been recognised as a writer of promise, Howard's End established him as a writer of substance; the adjective great was used to describe his work and invitations pursued him.

The period that followed was difficult for Forster. His repressed homosexuality stifled his creativity for he tired of pairing men and women together in his novels. Feeling lost and confused, he visited Edward Carpenter, a liberal freethinking social guru of his time. Forster felt the great man's magnetism; he also felt a touch on his bottom from the hand of George Merrill, Carpenter's lover. His creativity surged back and he wrote Maurice, a novel about homosexual love that Forster would not allow to be published in his lifetime.

After a brief spell looking after the paintings in The National Gallery, Forster travelled to Egypt with the Red Cross and fell in love with Mohammed el Ali, a young Egyptian tram driver. His experience in North Africa led to the publication of Alexandria - A History and a Guide and Pharaohs and Pharillion. Other journeys followed and in 1921 he was appointed secretary to the Maharajah of Dewas Senior in India. His experiences there led to the last of his novels, A Passage to India. Other works followed: short stories, essays, poems, a biography of Goldsworthy Lowes Dickinson, a writer; and interestingly a domestic biography of Marianne Thornton, his great aunt.

Forster possessed immense talent; he was widely recognised as the most distinguished man of letters of his generation, but he saw censorship and the widespread homophobia of his time as a threat to his craft. In 1928 he rallied public opinion to protest at the suppression of the lesbian novel The Well of Loneliness by Radclyffe Hall. He campaigned for civil liberties and also served as president of the British Humanist Society. With the outbreak of war Forster wrote essays or made broadcasts castigating the anti-Semitic violence of the Nazis, while at the same time advocating that loyalty to one's friends should take precedence over loyalty to one's country. In 1946 he was elected a Fellow of King's College, Cambridge, and later collaborated with Eric Crozier on the libretto of Benjamin Britten's Billy Budd. His death in 1970 was followed by the publication of Maurice.

STEVENAGE

Stevenage is Britain's first new town. Six residential areas were planned and built around Old Stevenage following the New Town Act in 1946. Each neighbourhood is self-contained and has its own schools, health facilities, shops, community centres and church. Bedwell was the first to be constructed, followed by Broadwater, Shepwell, then Chells, Pin Green and finally St Nicholas. There are also the newer developments of Poplars and Symonds Green.

In the immediate aftermath of war, the need to provide decent housing for returning soldiers and for those who had lost homes in the blitz was pressing. For others, the turn of events was disturbing: many homes and gardens were to be bulldozed, pubs and small-holdings were to be demolished. The destruction seemed heart-rending and foolish.

Campaigners strove to save as much of the gentle Hertfordshire countryside as possible and they appealed to Forster to join them. Forster was horrified by the scale of destruction about to descend upon the village and countryside he grew up in. He intervened and sparked a debate in the national newspapers on the merits of the new town development. Sadly, the involvement of the newspapers had the effect of dividing the participants in the debate along party political lines. A public enquiry followed that resulted in a decision to go ahead with the new town scheme. However concessions were made and an area of land to the north of Rook's Nest was reprieved. It comprised an area between Chesfield, Gravely and St Nicholas, and has become known as Forster's Country - an oasis in a new town desert - which, along with the old town, is the location of our walk.

LOCATION OF THE WALK, ACCESS AND PARKING:

By car: From J7 on the A1(M) follow the signs for Stevenage. With the motorway behind you go straight ahead at the first roundabout - on the A602 or Broadhall Way. At the next roundabout turn right onto the B197 and right again at the next roundabout. You are now travelling north on the B197 London Road. Go straight on at the next roundabout following the signs for the Railway Station and The Old Town. You should now be approaching the Six Hills Roundabout - just before you reach it you can see five small hills on your left (there are six but only five are now visible). These are the Roman tumuli which are thought to have inspired Forster to name the town in which Howard's End is located as Hilton. Drive on at the roundabout, past the station and turn right at the next roundabout into Fairlands Way, then turn left at the blue sign indicating long term parking. The car park belongs to the Aldi store - alas at a charge of £6. There are other cheaper and free parking options available but these impose time limits; the advantage of this car park is that it gives you plenty of time for the walk.

By train: probably the best way to travel so as to avoid all difficulties with parking. Stevenage is on the line between Kings Cross and Cambridge and trains are operated by First Capital Connect. If you come into Stevenage from the south you can see five small hills out of the east window (or the right hand side if you are facing the way the train is moving) just before you enter the station. These are Roman tumuli, of which there are six, and which are thought to have inspired Forster to name the town in which Howard's End is located as Hilton.

THE WALK

If you have parked in the Aldi car park, take the path that leads first to a small children's play area and then into an ornamental garden. Turn right at the far end by The Chequers Pub - you are now on what was once the Great North Way. If you look left towards Tesco's and the Railway Station you can see that its role as such a grandly named street is no more - the new town development saw to that.

If you have arrived by train, walk over the footbridge that spans the main road towards the theatre; go down the steps on the left just before you enter the theatre complex and walk towards the car park alongside the Tesco Superstore. If you imagine the car park as a square, you are now at the bottom left corner; at the top right hand corner there is another footbridge, i.e. on the opposite side of the car park. Walk over the footbridge and it will gradually merge into the road - the road that was once the Great North Way.

Whether you came by train or car you are now in the Old Town of Stevenage - or Hilton if you prefer. This is the road Charles Wilcox would have taken when collecting Helen's Aunt Juley from the station at the outset

The gateway to Forster Country.

of Howard's End; the road where both sought to slight the other; where both failed to connect. It is also the route that Margaret would have taken with her husband and the doctor when they were concerned - albeit with different motives - about Helen at the conclusion of the novel.

Walk along the main street: many of the mansions, coaching inns, cottages and shops would have been familiar to Forster in his childhood. At Simmonds the bakers, by the lawn mower shop, keep to the right and walk up Middle Row, a delightful parade of old fashioned shops and if you've time why not have your hair done at Howard's End Hairdressers?

Continue up the High Street, past the attractive Bowling Green on the left, past The Grange on the right with its blue plaque announcing, rather charmingly, that it was once the site of The Swan Inn - the first coaching inn where lovers stayed when eloping north to Greta Green - and past the timber framed cottages on the right whose long history included a stint as the workshop for Vincent H.R.D. motorcycles. Turn right just after Thomas Alleyne School, between the two brick pillars, onto the footpath. Forster describes the long chestnut avenue that lies before you as follows:

"Walking straight up from the station, she (Margaret Wilcox) crossed the village green and entered the long chestnut avenue that connects it with the church. The church itself stood in the village once. But it there attracted so many worshippers that the Devil, in a pet, snatched it from its foundations, and poised it on an inconvenient knoll, three-quarters of a mile away. If the story is true, the chestnut avenue must have been planted by angels. No more tempting approach could be imagined for the lukewarm Christian..."

Sadly many mature chestnut trees fell in the October storm of 1987 but replanting has taken place. In winter months you might be able to see the spire of the church "on an inconvenient knoll" through the leafless branches. In summer it is just about visible above the tree line. That spire, that church, is where we are heading for so put your best foot forward and stride on along the avenue, over the footbridge 500 yards further on, and uphill to the Church. Forster continues:

"At the church the scenery changed. The chestnut avenue opened into a road, smooth but narrow, which led into untouched country.....It strolled downhill or up as it wished, taking no trouble about the gradients, nor about the view which nevertheless expanded....Though its contours were slight, there was a touch of freedom in their sweep to which Surrey will never attain...."

With the rather unusual comparison with Surrey in mind perhaps you'd like to walk up the steps and through the churchyard that is attached to the beautiful Church of St Nicholas with its Norman tower and 15th century nave. Walk along the path on the south side of the church and keep going through several wooden arches in the cemetery beyond the churchyard, past the car park on the right and turn left when you reach Weston Road.

Walk up the narrow country lane; ignore the turning on the right and soon the white building of Rook's Nest Farm appears (where the rather

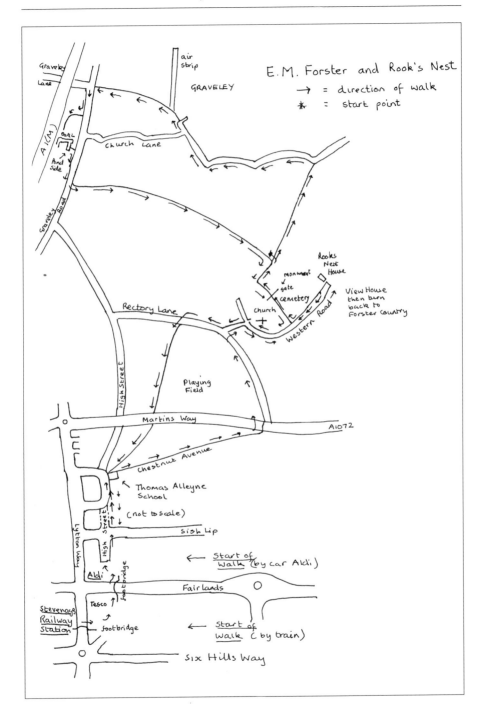

spooky Miss Avery lived). A few yards further on is a rosy-bricked house with dormer windows behind a rather tall and unkempt hedge. This is Rook's Nest, the childhood home of E.M. Forster who evoked the house and his love for it in Howard's End and later wrote of it as "…my childhood and my safety." Interestingly, the house had been known to Forster as Howard's after a family that had lived there for many years before his family took possession of it. When the Forsters moved they sold the house to long standing family friends called the Postons, who were the model for the Wilcox family in the book. Both Mr Poston and his son were called Charles, a rather unsavoury character in the novel. Elizabeth Poston enjoys a more sympathetic airing as the first Mrs Wilcox. Mrs Poston was also a writer and composer, although her work is not as well known as Forster's; perhaps her best known composition is a carol entitled Jesus Christ the Apple Tree.

Return now down the hill. The field on the right once belonged to the Forsters who rented it to the neighbouring farmer, Mr Franklyn. He had two boys, playmates for Morgan, and they would scamper around the barns together. There was a machine in one of them that had large wheels and was used for cutting hay. Young Frankie Franklyn used to climb inside one of the wheels and whirl around while Forster looked on admiringly, not daring to do the same.

Carry on down the hill past the farm and the cemetery. After three or four hundred yards there is a hidden footpath on the right that leads up some stone steps to a gate. Follow the path through the churchyard but instead of turning left to go towards the church, carry straight on. At the far end of the path there is a modern sculpture inscribed "Only Connect," taken from the subtitle of Howard's End. It commemorates the year 1994 when Forster country was first incorporated into the Green Belt.

Continue down the hill as the path emerges onto a vista of gently undulating fields and hedges. This is the last remaining farmland within the borough of Stevenage and is the beating heart of Forster Country. Turn right at the bottom by the signpost, follow the path as it curves left in front of a pylon then climb uphill. At the top turn right, keeping another pylon to your left. These pylons were erected in the 1950s and Forster rather neatly referred to them as "the naked ladies." Carry straight on at the T-junction ahead with the woodland to your right. The path eventually joins a road; turn left here and go down the lane, first through woodland, then alongside fields and meadows. Enjoy the fine view of the church nestling in amongst the rooftops of Gravely across the valley. Keep going downhill past the white timber framed cottages and turn right by the lamp post and telegraph pole. Pause and delight in this most picturesque view of Gravely Hall Farm (built in 1770) and St Mary's Parish Church.

Approach the setting and follow the track as it curves right in front of the church, then turn left onto the footpath about twenty yards further on, sign-posted Hertfordshire Way. Turn left again onto a track that leads over a bridge and walk uphill away from a private landing strip for aircraft and micro lights. At the top veer left, then right, effectively going straight on through an array of mouth watering fruit bushes. At the far end of the nursery, the path curves to the right but a gap will appear in the hedge, next to a holly bush. Go through the gap and down the steps to the road. Turn left, cross over and walk down towards the village.

Turn right up a gravely track on the outskirts of the village; and left at the top by a dark wooden building. You should now be walking southbound and parallel to the A1(M) - alas! Turn left into Oak Lane and down the hill, then right at the bottom into Pondside. You might wish to sit on one of the benches by the pond to take in the delightful village scene.

Next turn left along the alleyway that is just beyond the bench on the left by a white fence that leads alongside the Waggon and Horses Pub. Turn right when you emerge, cross the road and leave the village. Turn left just after a low brick wall by some bollards; keep to the right of the house on a footpath and walk to the far end of the field, then turn right and climb uphill. When the hedge ends, stride out across the fields and breathe in the stunning farmland vista that opens up in front of you: a testament to modern farming practice. Keep going for a fair old trot across the top of the hill, and when eventually you reach the hedge, turn right towards the electricity pylon. When the path joins with another, turn left and walk down the hill on the right side of the hedge alongside a plantation of young trees. Change sides when the space appears, continue downhill and turn right at the bottom by the pylon.

Walk along the bottom of the valley, keeping to the left of the path. When you reach the end of the field, turn left, uphill and re-enter the churchyard by Forster's sculptured commemorative stone. Turn right at the path that leads down to the church steps and onto the road once again. Walk down the hill towards the chestnut avenue but for want of variation on the return leg stay on the road as it bends round to the right. Several large, handsome houses border the road including The Priory on the left, once home to William Jowitt, a Liberal M.P. who served as Solicitor General in Churchill's wartime coalition and was appointed Lord Chancellor by Clement Attlee.

Keep going downhill and turn left onto a narrow footpath - one that bans cycling - that is opposite a steep-roofed bungalow called Crofton's Cottage. You will soon emerge onto some delightful parkland; take the pass underneath the main road further on and bear right as you ascend the other side, then left onto the tarmac path and immediately left again and enter a field. Head for the other side staying to the left of the children's play area, then right down to the main road where you turn left. You will no doubt have recognised that you are back on the Great North Way in Old Stevenage. If you came by train, cross over the footbridge at the far end of town, cross the car park and climb up the steps by the theatre and over the main road. If you parked next to the Aldi store, walk down the High Street and turn left into the ornamental garden by The Chequers Pub, thence to the children's play area and finally to the car park.

BIBLIOGRAPHY AND FURTHER READING:

Forster E.M. Howards End. New York: Book-of-the-Month-Club, 1995.
Forster E.M. A Room with a View. New York: Book-of-the-Month-Club, 1995.
Forster E.M. A Passage to India. New York: Book-of-the-Month-Club, 1995.

Walk 3:

GRAHAM GREENE'S BERKHAMSTED: 6 MILES

GRAHAM GREENE

Graham Greene, the creator of an exotic and exciting world famously termed Greeneland, was brought up in the more familiar location of home counties middle class suburbia. He found life at home so relentlessly boring that he took up Russian roulette as a distraction. In 1923, when aged 19, he found a revolver in the corner cupboard of a room he shared with his brother. There was also a box of bullets. He took both and made off to Berkhamsted Common. Having found a secluded spot, he took the gun from his pocket, slipped a bullet into one of the six chambers, and spun them round. He then placed the muzzle of the revolver into his right ear and pulled the trigger. Click!

Fortunately for his family and lovers of his work the chamber was empty, as it was on the other five occasions when he replayed this terrible game. Greene has described the moment when his finger pulled the trigger as being "accompanied by a surge of adrenalin through the system that dissipates the boredom." (Allain 1981). "One day," he described, "I disappeared onto the Common for my usual game of Russian roulette. I pulled the trigger once. I reloaded. A second time. Nothing. Then I put the revolver back in the drawer once and for all - I had become indifferent to my own death."

Greene's difficulties stemmed from his family's relationship within Berkhamsted School which he attended from the age of eight. His father was headmaster and his elder brother Raymond was a school prefect and later head of house. He felt himself a Quisling, an untrustworthy figure known to have dubious associates. He was surrounded by forces of resistance (the other boys) which he couldn't join without betraying his father and brother. Greene's father would ask him questions about the boys from time to time, and similarly the boys were ever curious about Graham's home life. He became adept at fielding these questions: he gave away only minor snippets of information and was amazed at the response they provoked. "My mother swept the carpet last night." "Really?" Innocuous statements aroused immense curiosity among the boys who seemingly had difficulty in imagining that teachers had to complete household chores in the same way as their own parents.

In Our Man in Havana Greene makes delightful use of his childhood experience when the hero, James Wormold, a mild-mannered vacuum cleaner salesman, is unwillingly recruited as a secret agent. Wormold is encouraged to provide information which he does by lifting illustrations from a vacuum cleaner manual and presenting them as drawings of secret weapons components to his spy master.

Greene loathed school: he felt an absence of privacy, the toilet doors could not be locked, the boys seemed never to stop farting and scatology pervaded the dormitories. Greene's problems came to a head one summer on the last day of the school holiday. He wrote a note saying that he had taken to the Common and would remain there until his parents agreed that he should not return to his prison (i.e. school). He overlooked how his parents were to communicate their agreement or disagreement to this ultimatum, left the note on the sideboard and ran to the hills. He felt liberated and enjoyed his rebellion up above Kitchener's Fields (now the cricket pitch). Later he was walking between the bushes when he came face to face with his sister Molly. He returned home with her. A family conference was called and his brother Raymond suggested psycho-analysis as a possible solution. His father, to his son's astonishment, agreed and Graham was diagnosed as a manic depressive.

It was while at school that Greene displayed the early signs of his talent for writing. A short story entitled The Tick of a Clock appeared in the school magazine and was later published by The Star newspaper for which he received the significant sum of £5. Later he wrote sentimental fantasies for The Saturday Gazette edited by a woman he met during his psycho-analysis.

After school, Greene went to Balliol College, Oxford. He joined the Communist Party in Paris but soon tired of the endless meetings. He offered his services instead as a propagandist to the German Embassy in London. The Germans quickly responded and Greene was provided with funds for a journey to French-occupied Germany. His mission was to ascertain information as to French future intentions over the creation of a separate Palatine republic. On his return Greene published an account of his findings in the Oxford Chronicle. At the same time he wrote to a right wing journal called The Patriot, offering to be their foreign correspondent and asked the French Embassy for contacts. It seems that he was about to embark on a life of espionage when the western powers met and thrashed out their differences: Greene's services were no longer required. Even so it was heady stuff for a nineteen year old.

Greene enjoyed the opportunity for solitude that Oxford provided and avoided becoming embroiled in college life. Evelyn Waugh, a contemporary, thought "that Greene looked down on us as childish and ostentatious. He certainly shared in none of our revelry." For Greene, just to have a room of his own brought immense satisfaction. In any event how could that student revelry compare with the thrill of receiving mysterious night time visits from Count von Bernstorff, the first secretary of the German Embassy, and his henchmen.

Greene wrote several articles, reviews, stories and poems that appeared in the student magazine Oxford Outlook and Oxford Poetry and in 1925 he published a thin volume of poems under the title Babbling April. Poor sales and dismal reviews followed. Greene himself was ashamed of the book and tried to prevent its circulation by buying all the printed copies.

Greene left Oxford with a degree in history, an unpublished novel and the acquaintance of Vivien, the woman he was to marry and the woman who introduced him to the Catholic faith. Work beckoned and after brief ventures with British American Tobacco and the Nottingham Journal he joined The Times as a sub-editor. He also started work on his second novel The Name of Action, then a third The Man Within. Four happy years later and feeling emboldened by the sales of 8,000 books, Greene resigned. His mentors at The Times were aghast that he should wish to and told him that if only he were patient, he might well become correspondence editor!

Graham and Vivien, now his wife, went to live in a Cotswold village where he ignored the rich tapestry of events that were taking place all around him. Instead he wrote Rumour at Nightfall, a story of the Carlist rebellion in Spain, which Greene had never visited. Disastrous reviews and sales of only 1,200 copies finally opened his eyes to the harsh realities of being a professional author. Stamboul Train followed; a book which in Greene's own words "are laden with the anxieties of the time and the sense of failure."

Even Greene's dreams revealed his anxieties - in one he relates that he was condemned to prison for five years and he woke depressed by the thought that he would not see his wife for another five years. The dream, however, provided him with the germ of an idea for his next novel, It's a Battlefield, a novel about spiritualism and incest.

Stamboul Train enjoyed some success but the poor sales of his other books meant that Greene had to look for other work. He applied for posts with The Times and The Catholic Herald but was turned down by both. Then Stamboul Train was chosen by the Book Society which led to sales of 10,000 copies. It was also made into a film by Twentieth Century Fox called Orient Express. His anxieties - or some of them at least - were over.

Greene diversified and wrote book and film reviews for The Spectator and The Times. The work obviously inspired him for A Gun For Sale followed in 1935 - a book which seems in many ways based on a film. It starts with two murders by a mysterious gunman and goes on to analyse the attractions and costs of evil.

The part of Greene's life that was to follow was immensely successful; his children Lucy and Francis were born and five novels were published in three years that were to establish him as a major author and a prodigious talent: England Made Me (1937), Brighton Rock (1938) and three in 1939 The Lawless Roads (set in Mexico which unlike Spain he had visited), The Power and The Glory and The Confidential Agent. He also wrote a travel book Journey Without Maps set in Liberia.

The outbreak of war brought Greene's latent talents for espionage and mis-information to the fore. He joined the SIS and was despatched to Sierra Leone. At first the plan was to send him to Liberia but someone at the ministry read his travel book and decided that he might not be welcome there. So he set off to Freetown and took on the role of a colonial policeman. He befriended the local Commissioner of Police Captain Brodie, who became the model for Major Scobie in The Heart of the Matter. In one colourful operation, Greene tried to set up a brothel and provide services for the Vichy Governed French Officers in the West Africa state in the hope that secrets and indiscretions might emerge. Alas this machiavellian scheme was never developed.

In 1943 Greene returned to work in counter intelligence first in St Albans, then in Portugal. He reported to Kim Philby and the two men became friends. Greene wrote the introduction to Philby's memoirs My Silent War, a work in which Philby praises Greene. The work involved providing Germany with disinformation through a double agent who pretended to have a network of spies working for him throughout England. The Germans believed his reports of troop movements and the like. His real usefulness came later in 1944 when he managed to convince the Germans that the anticipated invasion was an allied ploy.

After the war Greene was commissioned to write the screen play for a film set in Vienna, a city occupied by the four powers. The combined talents of Carol Reed, Orson Welles, and the haunting music of the zither played by Anton Karas, produced a pessimistic story of deception and drug trafficking that has been rated the Best British Film of the 20th Century by the British Film Institute.

His writing continued with many more publications including The Quiet American, The Comedians and Travels With My Aunt. In 1966 he moved to Antibes and later to Vevey, on Lake Geneva in Switzerland. In 1981 he was awarded the Jerusalem Prize, given to writers concerned with the freedom of the individual in society. He died in 1991 at the age of 86 and was buried in the cemetery at Corsier-sur-Vevey.

LOCATION OF THE WALK

By car: Berkhamsted is about 6 miles from junction 8 on the M1; take the A414 signposted Hemel Hempsted and the A4251 signposted Berkhamsted. It can also be reached from junction 20 on the M25, via the A41 signposted Aylesbury and the A4251 signposted Berkhamsted.

By train: there are up to four trains an hour from London Euston and Milton Keynes to Berkhamsted. The journey time in both cases is about 30 minutes.

PARKING

Free parking is available in Highfield Road and on payment in Water Lane Car Park in the centre of town between Tesco's and Sketchley's.

BERKHAMSTED

Berkhamsted is a town steeped in history with many Norman, Tudor and Victorian buildings but our purpose is to explore the more recent heritage of the town relating to Graham Greene. Fortunately the young Graham was resident in, educated at or ventured amongst the town's more interesting sites. The walk will take the reader through the centre of town, then on a climb across Berkhamsted Common before descending along the canal and back into town.

THE WALK

Perhaps the most appropriate starting point for the walk is Greene's birth-place and home until he was six. From the Water Lane car park, walk to the High Street, turn left then take the second turning right into Chesham Road. About one hundred metres up the road on the left is St John's, one of the boarding houses of Berkhamsted School where Graham's father was house-master. There used to be a small garden here and another across the road to which the family had access: now 1-4 Dean's Lawn. The young Greene used to imagine it was France and a family trip to the garden on Sundays meant crossing the road - or in Graham's eyes crossing the channel. Later, when a teenager, Greene often played truant to avoid games. On these occasions he would sneak further up Chesham Road and hide in a ditch adjacent to a lane that branched off into the countryside. There he would sit and read until it was time to return. Now go back down the hill to the High Street and turn right. There you will see Dean Incent's House, a fifteenth century building, once used as a public meeting place and probable birthplace of John Incent, a Dean of St Paul's and founder of Berkhamsted School.

On the other side of the High Street is a barber's shop that once housed W.H. Smith, the scene of Graham's dissolute beginnings for he occasionally stole books and magazines from the shop. Cross the road and keep to the left of St Peter's Church. The green behind the church is a graveyard, where Graham aged sixteen, read poems aloud from the Olde Yellow Book with a friend, both sitting on a gravestone with a sense of daring and decadence. His parents, who Graham was trying to provoke, were in their house: at this time a red brick building on the other side of the churchyard. Charles Greene had

The school house at Berkhamsted.

been appointed headmaster of Berkhamsted School and had moved into the School House in 1910 when Graham was six.

Climb the steps behind you and walk along the path between the church and the graveyard, down the steps at the far end and turn left into Castle Street. Many of the houses on the right hand side beyond Chapel Street used to be shops. There was a sweet shop, a jeweller, a pawn broker (who once declined Graham's attempt to pawn a broken cricket bat) and a shop owned by a woman who prepared tripe. Further down the road on the left is a square, half brick, half tiled, flat roofed building built by Charles Greene, that serves as the school sanatorium. Near here, Graham kept a kitchen garden, growing radishes and collecting snails which exploded into a foam when tipped into a bucket of salt water. Graham was encouraged and rewarded for his efforts with a small sum for every hundred corpses.

The sanatorium replaced a number of old alms houses, one of which was the disturbing scene of a suicide of a man who cut his throat; an event witnessed by a tender five year old Graham Greene.

Continue down the street, over the canal (you will have a chance to walk alongside the canal later) and turn left into Lower King's Road. Berkhamsted Station is now in front of you. The journey you have taken so far is probably that which Greene's character Castle took, albeit in reverse, in The Human Factor. Castle has returned home to Berkhamsted, he collected his bicycle and went:

A lock on the Bridgewater canal which a very young Graham Greene thought was the seaside.

"across the canal bridge, past the Tudor school, into the High Street, past the grey flint parish church...then up the slope of the Chilterns towards his small semi-detached house in King's Road."

Turn right under the railway bridge into Brownlow Road then right again into White Hill and to the fabulous ruins of Berkhamsted Castle, originally a wooden motte and bailey built by the Normans and the site where William the Conqueror received the crown of England.

As you go in, climb the steps to the top of a mound on the left. Face the castle and you will see a moat. Look behind you to your left and you will see another moat. There is a third inside the bailey, so an elaborate array of moats provided the castle with excellent defences. The castle and surrounding estates were owned by William's brother, Robert, Count of Mortaigne. In the twelfth century, it was rebuilt in stone by Thomas Beckett and later occupied by Edward, the Black Prince who fought at Crecy when only sixteen years old with many Berkhamsted archers. Greene often played here as a child and came to stare at an airship, that had landed here. It was captained by an old boy of the school and remained for several days on show. The event was photographed by a local stationer: the photographs were then converted into picture postcards and sold.

When you move on, turn left and walk alongside the railway line. Turn left at the junction 150 metres further on, ignoring White Hill. Follow the road round for four hundred metres. This road was the route taken by Greene when he escaped to the hills after leaving his parents his ultimatum. He describes the scene in A Sort of Life as follows:

"There was a wonderful sense of release from all the tensions and the indecision as I made my way up the long road lined with Spanish chestnuts from the ruined castle to the slope where the Common began. I had to hurry, for here on this open road I might have been intercepted, but the race against time was part of the excitement on that golden autumn day, with a faint mist lying along the canal, across the watercress beds by the railway viaduct and in the grassy pool of the castle. Then I was safely there, on the Common, among the gorse and bracken of my chosen battlefield."

Soon you will see a footpath sign on the right indicating Berkhamsted Golf Club. Go through the gate and up the hill under the canopy of beech trees. At the next gate follow the path that leads to the left hand house at the top of the ridge. At the top the path will veer round to the left and run parallel to a hedge. As you climb take a moment to enjoy the magnificent view of Berkhamsted nestling among rolling hills, meadows and pastures. The tall structure away to the left is the Bridgewater Monument, erected in 1832 to commemorate the 3rd Duke of Bridgewater and his pioneering work on British canals.

Follow the path all the way along staying close to the hedge. At the far end climb over a stile, then go through a kissing gate and turn left down through the woods to the road at the bottom. There is a concrete driveway on the other side of the road - ignore this - take instead the bridleway to the right of it by the wooden signpost. The bridleway will continue downhill through the woods to an intersection of footpaths. Go straight across and carry on up the hill. At the top, continue alongside a fence until it joins another path. Veer left to join the path which will soon broaden out into a track and go downhill. When the path forks left and right, take the left fork and traverse the hillside amid the ferns and enjoy the beautiful views over the valley. Ignore any paths on the left. The track will curve right and left and soon you will come to a bridleway with a signpost indicating that you are on part of the Grand Union Canal Circular Walk.

You are now on the southern edge of Berkhamsted Common. As a child Graham hated games but enjoyed running on the wide open spaces here. In solitude he could dramatize the loneliness and isolation that he felt being the son of the headmaster at a boarding school. He fantasised himself as the hero of John Buchan's Thirty-Nine Steps hiding out on the Scottish moors with every man's hand against him. Here he played his game of Russian roulette and another time picked and ate a bunch of deadly nightshade which he has described as having "a slight narcotic effect."

When you come to the post don't go on to the muddy track but carry straight on the wide grassy path to the left of the gorse bushes. Soon the path will split into two: take the narrow path branching to the left that runs first by ferns then between beech trees and gorse bushes. After a short distance there will be a post with a single blue arrow pointing straight on, then another with three. Keep straight on and enter the forest. There should be a house on the right. Veer left when you reach the driveway that comes down from the house,

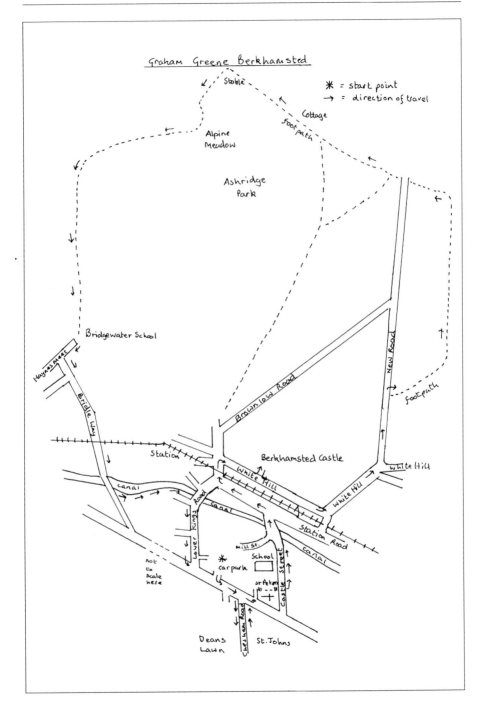

and later turn right as you approach the paddock. The path, now bordered with holly bushes on both sides, will curve right and a smaller, narrower path will appear on the left. Take this short path and climb over the style. This will lead you through the paddock next to a hedge. Keep going through gates and over styles down the hill, all the time staying close to the hedge.

At the far end of the paddock beyond an aluminium gate is the Alpine Ridge Meadow Nature Reserve, the banks of which in spring are laden with violets and primroses. Walk down into the valley then climb up the other side and after the next gate turn right and stay parallel with the trees until you reach the top of the hill. Follow the path as it veers round to the right and skirts the edge of a large field and the woods. Berkhamsted now lies ahead of you in the distance.

After a longish walk you will arrive at a gate and the path will descend alongside a wire mesh fence to a school. Turn right by the school onto the road then turn left at the junction into Bridle Way. Continue downhill and cross the grey railing bridge over the canal. At the end of the fence turn left and walk on the path that leads to the canal and turn right along the towpath.

Graham's innocent charm is revealed when as a very young boy he listened to the stories that his family told about the seaside at Littlehampton. He assumed that the place they were speaking of was a pile of sand in a timber yard by the canal; consequently he saw no reason to be excited at the prospect of going there.

Enjoy the stroll past the slow-moving barges; walk under two brick lined bridges and on to a third iron bridge that has been painted red and black and is just beyond a lock. Go up the steps by this bridge to the road above and turn right at the top. You are now in the Lower Kings Road. Continue to the traffic lights and turn left into the High Street. Water Lane and the car park behind Tesco's is further down on road on the left.

Should you wish to have some refreshments then I recommend the Attic Café on the fourth floor of the Home and Colonial Stores opposite Cresham Road. It is straight out of Greeneland. Finally, if you still have some energy, go further down the main road to the Easy Street Restaurant which is also the foyer to an excellent cinema that has been recently - and magnificently - renovated. Charles Greene once allowed his senior boys to go there for a special performance of the first Tarzan film. He had the mistaken impression that it was an educational film of anthropological interest. He was disappointed, but I rather imagine the boys were not.

BIBLIOGRAPHY AND FURTHER READING:

Greene, Graham. A Sort of Life. London: The Bodley Head Ltd, 1971.
Greene, Graham. Ways of Escape. London: The Bodley Head Ltd, 1980.
Greene, Graham. The Human Factor. London: The Bodley Head, 1978.
Allain, Francoise. The Other Man: Conversations with Graham Greene. London: The Bodley Head, 1983.

Walk 4:

SAINT THOMAS MORE, LORD CHANCELLOR

OF ENGLAND AND RESIDENT OF GOBIONS: 2 MILES

SAINT THOMAS MORE

Watching films made in the 1930s can make fascinating viewing for those interested in the changes that have taken place in our culture and attitudes over the last seventy years. The changes can occasionally seem quite striking: chauvinism, then seemingly commonplace, is now unacceptable in many societies, and it is difficult to understand the insensitivity of well-intentioned people of the time. If the changes over the last half-century or so are note-worthy, then over the last 500 years they are momentous. Take for example the attitude of John More, Thomas's father, towards women: he once said, "Marrying is akin to putting a hand into a sack of snakes and eels, seven snakes to the eel, and trying to draw the eel out without looking."

The image is disturbing. Even allowing for the custom of marrying to form alliances between states, or to build up estates and accepting that love was not considered, the quote to a modern reader seems monumentally unjust. John More is also quoted as saying that, "There is only one wicked wife in the world and every man knows she is his own."

Like father, like son, for Thomas's opinions were very similar. He routinely mocked and ridiculed women and only praised them to enhance the evil, ignorance or notoriety of a man with whom he was in conflict. "Even a woman," he seemed to be saying, "is better than this man."

Irreverence towards women was in stark contrast to the reverence shown towards the elderly. Throughout his life, even when in the exalted office of

Lord Chancellor, Thomas More greeted his father by going down on both knees and asking for his father's blessing. John More would then place both hands on his son's head as in the ritual of ordination.

Thomas was born in London in 1478 and went to St Anthony's School in Threadneedle Street. At the age of twelve he was sent to serve in the household of John Morton, The Archbishop of Canterbury and a man who was later to be an influential figure in the downfall of Richard III. Morton features in More's chronicle of the monarch, a chronicle that was plagiarised by William Shakespeare for his historical play. In due course Thomas left Morton and continued his education at Oxford.

The National Curriculum of the middle ages comprised The Seven Liberal Arts - the literary trio - or trivium - of Grammar, Logic and Rhetoric, which Thomas was taught at school, in addition to Latin; and the mathematical quartet - or quadrivium - of Geometry, Arithmetic, Astronomy and Music, which he studied at University.

More was a pious and obedient scholar with aspirations to be a priest, but ordination into the priesthood, then as now, required novices to take an oath of chastity. The oath challenges a biological imperative and is not to be lightly undertaken. Thomas yearned for the physical embrace of a woman so he acquiesced when his father suggested that he should study law. He left Oxford and headed for the Inns of Court in London.

Thomas was to regret the decision throughout his life. He did not forgive himself for bowing to secular temptation and frequently atoned for his weakness by beating himself with whips and wearing a hair shirt: a harsh scratchy garment worn next to the skin. Later he was horrified when Luther taught that priests and nuns should marry.

The curriculum at the Inns of Court included singing, harmony and dance, as well as the more conventional subjects of history, scripture, and the law of contracts and wills. It also included noble manners: the rituals and protocol that the nobility used to distinguish themselves from commoners. The subject, being taught to those with a bent for logic and oratory, raised some interesting philosophical points in debate. If nobles had to be taught to act nobly, could not anyone learn the subject? And could not anyone who behaved nobly, be considered noble?

Soon after qualification More married Jane Colt, the seventeen year old daughter of a prosperous Essex gentleman. Erasmus has written of marriage in a colloquy in which he tells of a young man who married a girl of seventeen. Modern scholars have assumed that the story is a true account of the relationship between Thomas More and Jane Colt. Richard Marius in his biography of Thomas More picks up the story:

"Her very simplicity impressed the youth because he imagine that he could train her to his match his own taste. He taught her literature and music, and when they had been to a sermon, he made her repeat the words of the preacher to see if she had understood them.

The girl rebelled! She answered her husband's insistence with tears, and sometimes she beat her head against the floor. The husband , unable to do anything with her, suggested a visit to her father in the country. Once there, the husband left her with her mother and sisters and went hunting with the father. He asked the question: What could he do to make his wife obey? The father counselled a good beating. The husband demurred.

The father did his part; he drew his daughter aside, and he reminded her of how ugly she was, how crude, how often he had feared that he could not find her a husband…The daughter went on her knees and begged forgiveness. She also fell on her knees before her husband and begged him to forgive her."

Thereafter she proved herself a chastened woman and the perfect medieval wife: she studied for an hour or two every evening, bore four children and died giving birth at the age of twenty three.

More often professed a lack of ambition in his public life but he enjoyed a meteoric rise through the great offices of State. He was elected to Parliament in 1504 when aged 22; and six years later was appointed Undersheriff of London. His diplomatic skills brought him to the notice of King Henry VIII, to help resolve a dispute concerning the trading of wool with Flanders. He was also part of the King's entourage at The Field of the Cloth of Gold. His service was rewarded with an appointment to the privy council and a knighthood. More further gained the King's favour by assisting him to write Defence of the Seven Sacraments, challenging Luther's basis for the schism from the Catholic Church. The piece has been described as "one of the most successful pieces of Catholic polemics produced by the first generation anti-protestant writers." It was dedicated to Pope Leo X, who rewarded Henry with the title Fidei Defensor.

The work was a repudiation of Lutherism. Lollardy, Lutherism and Protestantism all had roots in anticlericalism with an anger and frustration at the wealth and corruption enjoyed by the Catholic Church and the inadequacy of its ministers. Importantly, instead of simply looking to reform the Church, Luther and his followers were developing an alternative theology that made the Bible the sole authority for the Christian faith, rather than the Church and its hierarchy. They questioned the central teachings of the Church and some believed that the Church had no valid role to play as an intermediary between the individual and God. They therefore rejected the seven sacraments performed by priests (baptism, confirmation, confession, Eucharist, ordination, marriage and extreme unction) and anything which relied on the intercession of saints, such as praying to them, venerating them or even going on a pilgrimage. In the forthright words of Hawisia Mon, a convicted Lollard going on a pilgrimage served no purpose except to enrich priests "that be too riche and to make gay tapsters and proude ostlers."

In 1523 More was appointed Speaker of Parliament and in 1529, he was appointed Lord Chancellor in succession to Cardinal Wolsey. His professed position at court is perplexing: he disliked luxury and worldly pomp, and found the lies and flatteries of the court nauseating. That being so he felt unable to detach himself from the centre of power in the land for a more scholarly life at the family home, which he visited for two days each month.

More's first published work was a translation of a Latin biography of Picco della Mirandola by Giovanni Francesco. It was an interesting choice for Pico was a devout and learned lay writer. More admired him and saw him as a role model for his own life. After Pico's death, a priest reported having a dream in which Pico appeared suffused with fire for having refused a religious vocation. Dreams in the Tudor were thought by some to reflect the activities of the spiritual world. Given Thomas's regret at having turned his back on the Church he may have reflected gloomily on Pico's fate.

More's second publication was The History of Richard III. It is considered to be his finest work though not as influential as Utopia. The work was incorporated into Edward Hall's chronicle of 1543 as well as those of Holinshed in 1577. Richard III has long been suspected of the murder of the little Princes in the Tower though the evidence for his involvement is flimsy and based on hearsay. The real identity of the killers is one of the enduring mysteries of English history. More suspected Richard III and portrayed him as a tyrant. Shakespeare built on More's work in his play Richard III and the monarch's notoriety became complete. However, some believe that Richard III was a virtuous king who passed good laws in his brief reign and the real villain of the piece is More, who has wrongly slandered an innocent monarch.

A scandal in high places creates uproar whenever it occurs: in our current age or in December 1514 when Richard Hunne was found hanging by the neck in St Paul's Cathedral. The Church held that Hunne committed suicide. Londoners and a jury thought that the clergy murdered him. Hunne's death, however it was perpetrated, was the result of a personal tragedy, priestly greed and the intransigence of principled men in dispute.

The case concerned the sad death of Richard Hunne's five week old son Stephen, who had been baptized and was now to be buried. The Church traditionally required payment for the funeral service from the deceased, so the priest demanded the bearing sheet that the child had been wrapped in at his baptism. Hunne refused to hand over the sheet, so the priest sued him for it in an ecclesiastical court. Hunne fought the case, arguing that common law should take precedence over canon law, and in common law a deceased person cannot own property. The judges found in favour of the priest and Hunne was found hanged in a dungeon in St Paul's. The ecclesiastical court hounded Hunne after his death by adjudging him a heretic.

The practice of claiming payment for funeral services at the time of personal grief aroused great resentment among the public. There was also a widespread perception that the Church enjoyed an unwarranted degree of privilege. Hunne's death provoked rumblings of anti-Catholic sentiment to which More responded with a defence of the Church in his Dialogue Concerning Heresies. Some historians take a dim view of More's Dialogue, believing that it casts doubt on his integrity and that he distorted the facts to support the Church's view that Hunne was a heretic who committed suicide.

As we have seen More was a highly influential lawyer and Member of Parliament who acted for the King in Flanders. Whilst there, he rekindled a friendship with the noted Dutch scholar Erasmus. Erasmus had earlier visited England and stayed in More's London residence in Bucklersbury Street. He dedicated his book The Praise of Folly to More which became a Tudor best seller. The two men met frequently and their discourse led to More's most famous piece Utopia. Most historians believe that More started his book while in Flanders; some believe that he worked on the book or even finished it in Gobions.

Utopia may be considered the first work of the science fiction genre. It is a short work that tells the story of a traveller who has explored the New World and has found an idyllic island community. None of the islanders has a name, there is no private property, no private political discussion and no idleness. All must work in the fields for two years, all work for six hours a day and all live in similar houses that are exchanged every ten years. In many ways the island's social organisation resembles that of the Chinese communist regime. We might recognise life there dispiriting; More saw it as spiritually uplifting.

It was the manner of his death that has led to More becoming such an important historical figure. The upheavals of the Church following Henry's break from Rome led to Parliament passing The Act of Supremacy, in which to refuse to accept the king as head of the Church of England was high treason. More refused; he was charged and imprisoned in the Tower where he continued to write. Appropriately his works were called Treatise on the Passion and Dialogue of Comfort Against Tribulation. The latter tells of a man facing imprisonment and death who is preparing himself for the ordeal to come. Here is a sample:

Yea, I daresay almost every good Christian man would very fain this day that yesterday he had been cruelly killed for Christ's sake — even for the desire of heaven, though there were no hell. But to fear while the pain is coming, there is all our hindrance! But if, on the other hand, we would remember hell's pain into which we fall while we flee from this, then this short pain should be no hindrance at all. And yet, if we were faithful, we should be more pricked forward by deep consideration of the joys of heaven, of which the apostle saith, "The passions of this time be not worthy to the glory that is to come, which shall be showed in us."

In 1535 More was convicted for his steadfast defence of the indissolubility of Henry's marriage to Catherine of Aragon and the supremacy of the pope. More had used the time in prison well, he was prepared for his death as his writing reveals. His last words on the scaffold were "I have been the King's good and loyal servant, but God's first."

A walk in the woods on The Gobions Estate.

THE GOBIONS ESTATE AND THOMAS MORE

Thomas never owned the estate at Gobions. John More, his father, assigned the property to trustees for the use of his fourth wife Alice in the event of his death, and was to be passed on to Thomas after her death. After Thomas's execution, his lands were forfeited to the Crown. As long as Alice lived, the property was safe from forfeiture but she could nor live forever. She died in 1550 and the estate was duly relinquished. Edward VI granted the freehold to Princess Elizabeth, supposedly for the duration of her life. Edward ruled for a very short period and on his death, Mary seized the crown and the land at Gobions. After her death, Elizabeth inherited the throne and the estate, the latter of which she leased to Margaret Knowles. Towards the end of the 16th century, the property reverted again to the More family, who retained it for the most part of the 17th century.

GOBIONS AND THE SPRING

In late April and early May there is scarcely a finer place to walk in Hertfordshire: the land abounds with bluebells and celandines to provide a visual feast and an intoxicating bouquet. Take a tip and make an entry in your diary for the last weekend of April or the first in May.

LOCATION, ACCESS AND PARKING:

By car: leave the M25 at J24 for the A111, direction Potters Bar. At the traffic lights turn right on to the A1000, direction Hatfield. As you leave Potters Bar turn left for Brookman's Park at Hawkshead Road. When you enter Brookman's Park, take the second right which is Moffats Lane. At the top of the hill, there is an access road to the estate on the right between house numbers 88 and 94, by a black metal post. It looks rather like a private drive but don't be put off. Go down the access road which will soon open up into a car park.

By train: Gobions is a short walk from Brookman's Park Railway Station. Trains run regularly between Moorgate and Welwyn Garden City via Brookman's Park. When you leave the station, turn right and bear right at the green in the centre of the village. Turn left into Moffats Lane. Gobions can be reached via an access road between house numbers 88 and 94.

THE WALK

Leave the car park and stride out across the open parkland, staying parallel to the line of houses at the top of the hill. Maintain a distance of about thirty yards from the garden fences and enjoy the view of the lake below and the woodland all around. As you approach the trees at the far end of the parkland, a track will gradually come into view. Enter the woods via the track, still maintaining a parallel line with the houses. After 150 yards or so, the track will veer to the right, then left, and will gently descend. Thirty yards further on there is an intersection. The paths are not always easily seen, but the junction is by a large horse chestnut tree. Turn right and follow the track downhill through the woods.

At the bottom of the hill by the lake turn left - there should be no difficulties now - and keep going until you reach a kissing gate. Go through the gate and enter the Gobions Wood Nature Conservation Area. Pause for a moment by the wooden gates left and right of the path five yards further on. The meadow on the left was once the site of a small manor house, More Hall, owned by Sir John and Lady Alice More, Thomas's parents. The house was much improved by a blind 18th century resident named Sir Jeremy Sambrooke, one time Lord Mayor of London. Sir Jeremy also built a bowling green, a canal and planted a formal garden on the estate.

Carry on down the hill, cross a footbridge at the bottom and veer left. Turn left again at the T-junction a few yards further on and wander through what is arguably the most delightful woodland in the county. On the right are the overgrown and derelict remains of Sambrooke's ornamental lake. At the end of the lake, there is an arched bridge, once part of the canal system that has long fallen into disrepair. Thomas More's Utopia springs to mind, here is a short description of it:

"There goeth a bridge over the river made not of piles or of timber, but of stonework, with gorgeous and substantial arches......They also have another river which indeed is not very great. But it runneth gently and pleasantly. For it riseth even out of the same hill that the city standeth upon....And because it riseth a little without the city, the Amaurotians have enclosed the head-spring of it with strong fences and bulwarks....This is done to the intent that the water should not be stopped, nor turned away, nor poisoned, if their enemies should chance to come upon them."

Walk to the end and pause on the track by the wooden fence some five yards from the green footbridge. If you look along the track to the right, you may be able to make out The Folly in the distance. If you look to the left, you will see the meadow that was the site of More Hall. The track once led from The Folly to the manor house. More historians with an interest in the estate are of the view that Sambrooke constructed The Folly; some locals are of a different persuasion. They have it that it was built by Thomas More to welcome Henry VIII on the occasion of a royal visit to the Chancellor's Hertfordshire home. Perhaps even more fanciful is the gossip that a farthing lies under every brick!

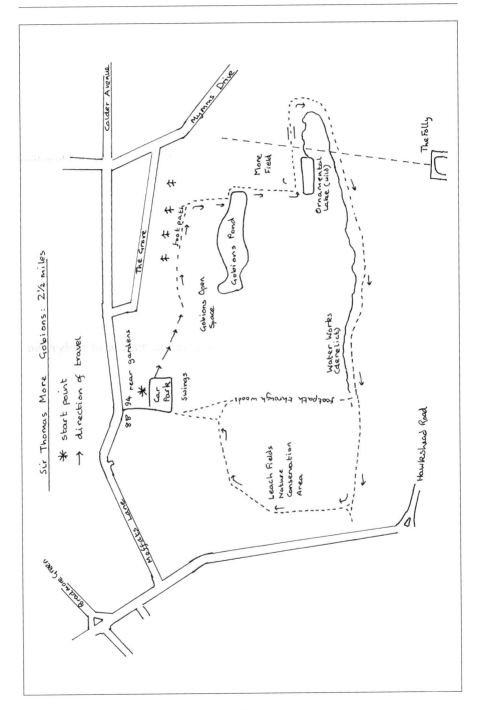

Continue the walk over the green wooden footbridge and follow the path as it runs alongside the stream. Ignore the first path on the right, instead thread your way carefully over exposed tree roots, all the while staying close to the stream. After 300 yards the stream will turn right as will the path, through a cluster of tall pine trees. Follow the path between fallen trees and over a small footbridge. Soon the stream will diminish in size to a small brook and will flow right next to the path.

When you reach an open field on the left that is bordered by a barbed wire fence, turn right and follow the path uphill through the woods. The path leads to the top of the hill and through a gap of felled trees. Follow it down the other side. At the bottom The Folly will be easily visible and now on your left. Ignore the track to the right but keep going straight on the narrow path that lies next to a ditch, that in turn lies next to a barbed wire fence. Turn left

The Folly At Gobions.

by an upturned tree and cross over another footbridge a few yards further on, then another and enjoy a different view of the ornamental lake.

Soon there is another bridge on the right that crosses the lake. Your route takes you straight on, but you might like to walk half-way across the bridge and in so doing, have a better view of some original features of the lake and canal.

Return to the path, turn right and walk over the next bridge, then up some wooden steps, then over another bridge. Eventually you will come to a fork: take the right hand fork and go down some steps. The path will lead through some dense growth and a ditch will come into view on the right. For those with an interest in industrial archaeology, the derelict ruins on the right housed the sewerage systems that provided Brookman's Park with clean water in the 1920s.

Soon there will be four footbridges in quick succession: go straight over the first two, , turn right at the third and immediately left at the fourth. The path emerges from the woods onto the delightful Leach Fields. Carry straight on, keeping the hill to your right. After 100 yards, turn right by a wooden gate and climb uphill as the path runs parallel to a line of trees on the left. At the fork at the top, veer left through the gap in the trees, then turn right and continue the steady uphill climb. After 300 yards or so, turn left through the gate next to the Gobions Woodland Trust sign, then aim for the far right hand corner of the next field. Walk through the gap in the trees that will appear as you approach. You will emerge by some children's swings; turn left just beyond them and walk uphill to the car park.

BIBLIOGRAPHY AND FURTHER READING:

Marius, Richard. Thomas More. London: J.M. Dent , a division of The Orion Publishing Group, 1985.
Chambers, R. W. Thomas More. London: Jonathan Cape, 1935.
More, Sir Thomas. Utopia. Ware: Wordsworth Editions, 1977.
More, Sir Thomas. Dialogue of Comfort Against Tribulation. 1534.

Walk 5:

GEORGE ORWELL, WALLINGTON

AND ANIMAL FARM: 3 MILES

GEORGE ORWELL

George Orwell, or perhaps more accurately Eric Arthur Blair, was born into the British Raj in 1903 at the northern Indian village of Motihari. His father, whom Orwell, either ironically or with precision, described as lower-upper-middle class, was an opium agent in the Indian Civil Service. As such he was able to provide a privileged and fairly pleasant existence for his family. They returned to England in 1907 and Orwell was sent to a number of public schools, including Eton, for his education. In his final year examinations he finished 138th out of 167 pupils - a position that must give hope to most of us.

Blair sought work that involved travel and action, and he found it in the role of a Burmese policeman. He also found the reality of policing the Empire was very much more challenging than he had imagined. He was frequently baited, insulted and jeered at by hostile Buddhist monks, who seemingly had nothing better to do than stand on street corners and deride Europeans. He grew to despise the locals: in frustration he hit servants and coolies with his fist and thought that the greatest joy of the world would be to drive a bayonet into a Buddhist priest's guts. In more reflective moments he saw his job as an instrument of imperialist tyranny and generally empathised with the views of his tormentors.

Early one morning Blair received a call requesting him to deal with an elephant that had rampaged through a bazaar. He collected his gun and some cartridges then set off. Various people stopped him on the way but were vague as to the elephant's progress. However, on noticing the gun, they joined him on his march. En route, he came across instances of damage and upheaval that the elephant caused: upturned fruit stalls, the trampled bazaar and a man who had been trodden to death. More and more people joined him until he arrived at a paddy field: he saw the elephant tearing up bunches of grass, beating them against his knees to clean them and stuffing them in his mouth. The elephant had experienced an attack of must which was now wearing off. It was a tame elephant so there was little for Blair to do. Yet there were now two thousand people watching him. He felt that if he walked away he would be laughed at so he shot the beast. He shot it five times for no other reason than to avoid the ridicule of the on-lookers. Blair walked away. He could not bear to watch the creature's agony. The elephant took half-an-hour to die. The crowd stripped the carcass of meat and ate well that night.

Blair wrote an essay of the experience in which he describes his reaction to the shooting: "And it was at this moment….that I realised the futility of the white man's dominion in the East. Here was I, the white man with the gun,…seemingly the leading actor in the piece; but in reality I was only an absurd puppet, pushed to and fro by the will of those yellow faces behind…….And my whole life, every white man's life in the East, was one long struggle not to be laughed at."

A chastening experience and desperate words. Blair resigned in 1928 and returned to Europe. He cleaned dishes in the Paris slums; then lived among the beggars and tramps in the East End of London, living in the main on tea and two slices of bread and margarine. He wanted to find out if the British (and presumably the French) treated the poor of their own country in the same way as they treated the Indians and Burmese. By and large they did. He wrote of his experiences in "Burmese Days" and "Down and out in Paris and London" under the pseudonym of George Orwell.

The choice of Blair's pseudonym was based on his affection for England - albeit a challenging affection. George was after both the patron saint and the monarch of the time; and Orwell, after the River Orwell in Suffolk - a place he loved to visit.

Later Orwell worked as a hop picker in Kent and as a schoolteacher, which provided him with experience for his novel "A Clergyman's Daughter." (1935) A later role as a book seller in Booklover's Corner in South

End Green, Hampstead also helped his writing in "Keep the Aspidistra Flying" (1936).

In 1936, Orwell moved to Wallington an in June and married Eileen O'Shaughnessy in the parish church. He opened a shop selling groceries to the villagers and sweets to their children; he clattered away on his typewriter whenever the shop was unattended. He was commissioned by The Left Book Club and Victor Gollancz to write "Road to Wigan Pier" (published 1937), a bitter polemic of working class life in the bleak industrial heartlands of Yorkshire and Lancashire. It has two sections: a highly readable and illuminating account of the lives of coal miners in the first, and a discussion of the negative aspects of socialism in the second. Orwell's socialism really did seek an improvement in the conditions of the working class, and not political change for its own sake.

After Wigan Pier Orwell went off to Spain to report the civil war. Whilst there, he responded to the call to arms and joined the European socialists in the fight against Franco's fascism. In May 1937 he was hit in the neck by a sniper's bullet. He was partially paralysed and temporarily lost his voice. He also developed a phobia of rats whilst in hospital with a poisoned hand, a phobia he enshrined in a later work "Nineteen Eighty-Four". On his return Orwell wrote of his experiences in "Homage to Catalonia".

The villagers of Wallington seemed to take his exotic existence into their stride, though perhaps laconically, Orwell described his activities in Spain as 'only burning catholic churches' when challenged by the local vicar.

In 1938 Orwell became ill with tuberculosis and spent the winter in Morocco, where he wrote "Coming up for Air" (1939). When war broke out he was declared unfit for active service, but served in the Home Guard and worked for the BBC. In 1943 he began writing "Animal Farm." The book was based on his observations of village life in Wallington and told, in fable form, of Stalin's betrayal of the Russian Revolution. It was published in 1945 and established Orwell as an author of international repute.

In 1944 Eileen died during a routine operation. Orwell moved with his newly adopted son Richard to the remote Hebridean island of Jura, where he worked on "Nineteen Eighty-Four" (1948). The book was set in a totalitarian future and introduced many phrases to the language such as 'big brother is watching you,' 'newspeak,' 'doublethink,' and 'room 101' which has come to prominence recently with the naming of a TV series.

Orwell's health deteriorated and in 1949, knowing he was close to death, he married Sonia Bronwell - a woman who had been the inspiration for the bossy Julia in Nineteen Eighty-Four. His marriage was more to secure a literary executor than a companion for his last days. He died on 21st January 1950.

LOCATION AND PARKING

At the time of writing this piece a new by-pass is about to open that takes traffic around Baldock. If travelling north on the A1(M), stay on the new by-pass after signs to Baldock. Turn off at the next junction, signposted to Wallington. Keep following the signs and after a short stretch across country, you will drive down the hill into the village. Turn left into The Street, where free parking is available on the left hand side on the road opposite the village hall.

There are no public transport links to the village. The nearest railway stations are at Ashwell and Morden or Baldock, both approximately three miles away with regular services into Kings Cross and Cambridge.

THE WALK AROUND WALLINGTON
AND A JOURNEY THROUGH ANIMAL FARM

The car park opposite the village hall once belonged to a pub and if you peer closely at the wooden shed you will see an old sign to that effect. Turn right and walk up the hill. The whitewashed house on the right used to be The Plough Public House and beyond it, number 2 Kitts Lane, is George Orwell's old house. The cottage could grace the pages of any lifestyle magazine with its thatched roof and distinguished heritage. When George moved in, it was very different. The roof was made of corrugated iron that amplified the weather report when it rained. The lavatory outside was linked to a cesspit that blocked up if the family failed to use the best lavatory paper on the market. "The best brand is Jeyes paper, which is 6d a packet," Orwell wrote to a friend. "The difference is negligible; on the other hand a choked cesspit is a misery."

Orwell ran the village shop from here: his takings of around thirty shillings (or £1.50) were enough to cover the rent of 7/6d (37½p) and his living expenses. He preferred it to his previous job selling books in Hampstead, though he was concerned about pilfering by the village children and drilled four holes into a door through which he could keep an eye on them.

Orwell used to rent the green opposite his house where he grazed his pigs, geese and a goat called Muriel. Interestingly a goat of the same name features in Animal Farm: she's the one who reads the ever-changing commandments to Clover, one of the two shire horses. In Wallington, a dray, pulled by two shire horses, delivered beer to The Plough; and Orwell would have had ample time to observe the animals from his house. The landlord of The Plough was Alfred Ridley, who is thought to be the inspiration of "a fat, red-faced man in check breeches and gaiters, who looked like a publican." This is the description of the man who "… stroked the nose of Mollie, the dainty mare who deserts the farm to wear ribbons, eat sugar and pull the trap."

Orwell's house in Wallington now thatched, originally with a corrugated iron roof.

Walk up the hill in the direction of Sandon. The black wooden building on the left is Manor Farm, mistakenly thought by many to be the model for Animal Farm. It does, however, feature in the book in a number of ways. First there is the name - in the book Manor Farm is renamed Animal Farm when the animals have taken over. Here in Wallington, the farmer did keep pigs, who are the leading characters of the book; the farmer also tried to erect a wind generator that fell down in bad weather. The Manor Farm that Orwell knew eventually failed and the farmer spent his days at The Plough bemoaning his luck in much the same way as Jones does in Animal Farm.

Continue up the hill past the pond and turn right. The dark buildings at the top are the outbuildings of Bury Farm that Orwell used as his model for Animal Farm. The whitewashed farmhouse on the right is where Farmer Jones, and later Napoleon, "slept between sheets in a bed." Orwell's Animal Farm, as with Bury Farm "had a cart track to the main road and could be reached by a drive up from the village." The store shed (the tall tower to the right is a later addition) is large enough to take many animals and five men described during the evening of the revolution as follows:

"At last they could stand it no longer. One of the cows broke in the door of the store shed with her horns and all the animals began to help themselves from the bins. It was just then than Mr Jones woke up. The next moment he with his four men were in the store shed with whips in their hands, lashing out in all directions."

Return a few yards down the hill and up to the village church. George married here in June 1936 soon after he moved into the village. Many of the pews were made in the 15th century. The enclosed pew on the right next to the pulpit is where the groom traditionally awaits his bride on their wedding day. You might imagine George nervously emerging as his beautiful bride arrived.

Turn right as you leave the church and right again through the gate, alongside a ditch and a brick wall. Follow the path as it veers to the left whereupon you should see a signpost to Wallington Common. Keep going as it curves left again, then right along a countryside avenue bordered on both sides by coppiced trees and hedges. Ignore the paths left and right. Soon you will reach an intersection by a post with blue and yellow arrows. Go straight on in the direction of the blue arrow.

Wallington Village Green where Orwell kept a goat called Muriel.

The path leads you into the Wallington Common Nature Reserve. Continue through the woodland, weaving a little with the path, and pass the dark post with the blue arrow and number 4 inscribed. When you emerge from the woods, keep going straight on alongside an open field with a hay barn in the middle distance on your left.

Soon a private drive will cross your path; go straight on into a tunnel of trees. The tunnel comprises sloe, elder, hawthorn, holly and oak, and is bordered by a field on the right and a meadow on the left. At the far end of the meadow, there are two bungalows where the path will steer to the left, and then merge with a gravel public byway. Turn left and walk alongside the Leylandii hedge. Go straight on when the path turns right into a farmyard; continue past the black wooden hay barn and veer slightly right onto the chalky white track. There should be a hedge on your right and a hay meadow on your left. Keep going past a fenced enclosure until you arrive at a half-tiled, half-thatched, whitewashed, stone-clad cottage on the edge of a small

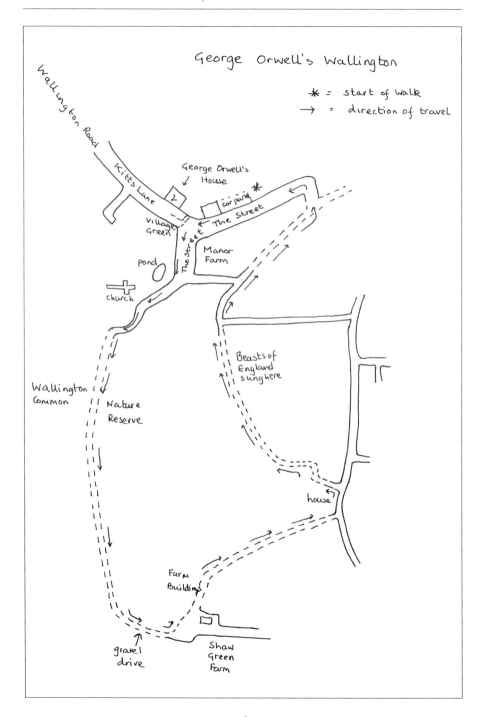

George Orwell's Wallington

✳ = start of walk
→ = direction of travel

Wallington Road

Kitts Lane

George Orwell's House

2

car park

The Street

Village Green

The Street

Manor Farm

Pond

church

Beasts of England sung here

Wallington Common

Nature Reserve

house

Farm Buildings

gravel drive

Shaw Green Farm

hamlet. Turn left just past the cottage along a dive between two thatched cottages. When the drive curves round to the right, keep going straight on by a hedge with a huge open field on your left.

When the hedge turns 90° to the right, stride out across the field in the direction of an oak tree. As you walk, a stile on the far side should come into view. Aim for the stile then continue by the fence and veer right as it descends gently down a small hill. Keep going up the other side; ignore the first stile then climb over the second one on the right a few yards further on. You should now be walking alongside a hedge with open fields descending down into a valley on your right. Eventually you'll reach an intersection of footpaths, when you do pause for a moment and look to your left. You'll see another view of Bury or Animal Farm. Where you are standing now is my best guess as to the spot where the Animals of Animal Farm came out to sing their anthem Beasts Of England for the last time. See if you agree from Orwell's description:

> *"The animals huddled about Clover, not speaking. The knoll where they were lying gave them a wide prospect across the countryside. Most of Animal Farm was in their view - the long pasture stretching down to the main road, the hayfield, the spinney, the drinking pool, the ploughed fields where the young wheat was thick and green, and the red roofs of the farm buildings with the smoke curling from the chimneys……..*
> *As Clover looked down the hillside her eyes filled with tears."*

Orwell must have been a romantic at heart! Continue straight across the intersection, keeping the hedge to your left and enjoy the views across the valley. Can you see the grey roofed house with two chimneys? This is thought to be the model for Mr Pilkington's Foxwood Farm described as a "large, neglected, old-fashioned farm, much overgrown by woodland, with all its pastures worn out and its hedges in disgraceful condition." Mr Pilkington himself is described as "…an easy-going gentleman farmer who spent most of his time in fishing or hunting according to the season." Mr Pilkington and his farm are thought to be an allegory for the western allies in the book.

Carry on as the path joins with the road and enters Wallington. When the road bends to the left, go straight on and walk along the public bridleway and down the hill. At the bottom turn left onto a grassy path which will shortly merge with a road that veers to the left and takes you up to the car park and the starting point of our walk.

EPILOGUE

Our closing paragraphs in this chapter are devoted to the varying allegory of Mr Whymper - he is the solicitor who visits Animal Farm on a weekly basis to receive his instructions and who acts as an intermediary between the Farm and the outside world. The allegory pertains to visiting dignitaries who were given the red carpet treatment and guided away from the grim realities of starvation in Communist Russia. Chapter VII of Animal Farm relates to the bitter realities of the world in 1933, Whymper is thought to represent George Bernard Shaw who features in the following chapter.

Orwell writes,

"Hitherto the animals had had little or no contact with Whymper on his weekly visits; now, however, a few selected animals, mostly sheep, were instructed to remark casually in his hearing that rations had been increased. In addition, Napoleon ordered that the almost empty bins in the store-shed to be filled with sand, which was then covered up with what remained of the grain and the meal. On some suitable pretext Whymper was led through the store-shed and allowed to catch a glimpse of the bins. He was deceived, and continued to report to the outside world that there was no food shortage on Animal Farm."

The Orwellian scholar Nigel Colley has written a detailed and informative piece on the allegory of Animal Farm at the following web site: colley.co.uk/ garethjones/soviet_articles/orwell. He writes:

"Now Whymper is obviously George Bernard Shaw who with Lord and Lady Astor were led by the nose to see model Collective farms in 1931, on the occasion of Shaw's 75th Birthday. ...... After dictator Josef V. Stalin the starving Russians most hate George Bernard Shaw for his accounts of their plentiful food."

Shaw and Orwell were contemporaries and neighbours, both prominent writers with a critical view of the class structure of their age. I have yet to find evidence of Shaw's awareness of Orwell's assumed critical portrayal of his naïvity.

BIBLIOGRAPHY AND FURTHER READING:

Orwell, George. Inside the Whale and other essays. London: Penguin Books Ltd, 1957.

Orwell, George. Animal Farm. London: Penguin Books, 1951.

Orwell, George. Down and Out In Paris and London. London: Penguin Books, 1940.

Orwell, George. Nineteen Eighty-Four. London: Penguin Books, 1954.

Walk 6:

GEORGE BERNARD SHAW AND HIS BELOVED

VILLAGE OF AYOT ST LAWRENCE: 4 MILES

GEORGE BERNARD SHAW

To his public George Bernard Shaw was a prolific writer, prominent socialist, orator and vegetarian. To his neighbours he was a much more complex character: occasionally warm-hearted, generous and welcoming whilst at other times he seemed shy and withdrawn, a touch mean and straight talking almost to the point of rudeness. Many of these paradoxes may have been the result of the adulation that was showered upon him for in the first half of the twentieth century, he was a much sought after celebrity, pursued by the paparazzi of his time.

Shaw daily received a huge sack of fan mail: invitations to speak, requests for donations and to inscribe various books. He replied to very many of his correspondents and hence struck up a relationship with Jisbella Lyth, who ran the village post office. Shaw wrote orders for his stamps on a post-card which she was able to sell to his adoring fans for 10/6d, and later three guineas as his fame grew. Jisbella was the inspiration for the heroine in the play "Village Wooing," which tells the story of an upper class, educated travel writer who meets a chatty telephone operator on a cruise ship. Despite his crabby reluctance, he is gradually drawn into conversation with her and the couple eventually marry. They settle together in a shop which he purports to manage. The play draws on the social mores of the time that prevented people of different social backgrounds from enjoying relationships. It also suggests that Shaw had a soft spot for the local postmistress.

The old post office in Ayot St Lawrence and home to Jisbella.

Shaw was born in Dublin in 1856. He wrote affectionately of his childhood, especially his relationship with his father who, on seeing his young son pretending to smoke his pipe, earnestly entreated the boy never to follow his example in any way. His father's sincerity obviously impressed the young Shaw for he never smoked, shaved or consumed alcohol. His mother sang and played the piano, and when Shaw was seventeen, she left her husband and son and moved to London. Shaw followed three years later.

Shaw's first play was "The Widower's House." Others followed but his first real success was "The Devil's Disciple" in 1897. In 1904 "John Bull's Other Island" was performed at The Royal Court Theatre - King Edward VII attended and laughed so much that he broke his seat. The ensuing publicity ensured the play had a good run. Other successes followed, notably "Pygmalion" and "St Joan." Then in 1915, Shaw wrote a manifesto entitled

"Common Sense about the War." He put forward an unpartisan view of the conflict and suggested that in certain circumstances, servicemen might be wise to shoot their officers. Unsurprisingly, the establishment took a dim view. Perhaps his comments reflected the repressed feelings of too many of his adopted compatriots for comfort. In any event, his work lost popularity.

After the war, Shaw enjoyed a revival with "Arms and the Man", and in 1925 he was awarded the Nobel Prize for Literature. He spent the prize money on publishing an English edition of the works of the Swedish playwright August Strindberg. In later years Shaw agreed to many of his plays being filmed - provided that he retained control over the script. His talent blossomed in the new medium for in 1938 "Pygmalion" was filmed and Shaw won an Oscar for Best Screenplay.

Shaw's legacy as a writer is well known. Less so are his political and social achievements: he was a founder member of the Fabian Society, an organisation dedicated to transforming Britain into a socialist state, and which founded the London School of Economics and the Labour Party. He also tried to establish a new alphabet of 138 characters, arguing that the existing alphabet was archaic and inefficient. Sadly for the world's English speaking schoolchildren, the idea has not proved as fruitful as some of his other ventures.

Shaw remained irascible to the end, neither holding his tongue nor his pen. He died in 1948 while pruning an apple tree in his garden and something of Ayot St Lawrence died with him. He was missed by many but his spirit lived on: in 1958 the new musical production "My Fair Lady" won huge acclaim in London and New York. The musical was inspired by "Pygmalion," which in turn was inspired by his mother's experience - that of an Irish woman with a funny accent in London.

LOCATION AND PARKING

From A1(M) junction 4 or M1 junction 10, take the B653 and follow the signposts to Wheathampstead, then to The Ayots, and finally to Shaw's Corner.

If you are combining your walk with a visit to Shaw's Corner, now owned by The National Trust, there is free parking available in the grounds of the house. Otherwise roadside parking is available in the village, in the vicinity of the telephone box and the old church.

SHAW'S CORNER

In 1902 the house at Shaw's Corner was built as a rectory for the parish of Ayot St Lawrence. As you wander around the village you may soon find yourself in sympathy with the view of the Church at the time, that the house was far too grand to house a vicar for such a small community. Consequently, in 1906 it was placed on the market and Shaw, being much attracted to the tranquillity of the area, bought it. He moved in with his wife. The Shaws' marriage was never consummated - he was 42 when he wed, the same age as his wife. He has explained that he was of an age when he was able to marry without seeming to do so for money, and his wife without seeming to be driven by sex starvation.

Shaw had a small wooden summerhouse installed in the beautiful gardens. It was little more than a shed but it was fitted with a telephone and electricity. Rather delightfully, it could be turned to enable the sun to shine in when he was working. Following recent restoration, the summerhouse can again be turned. Visitors can also view a range of writing implements there of the type that Shaw would have used to write his later plays.

THE WALK

From the car park at Shaw's Corner, turn right and walk to the T-junction 100 yards ahead. Turn left and north, past the Old Rectory on the right: a lovely, rambling Grade II listed building that now offers bed and breakfast facilities to visitors to the area. In Shaw's day, the house was converted into flats and Shaw called on all the new residents when they moved into the village. Further on, just before the road turns to the right, look to the left at the end of the hedge and enjoy the view of the new village church across the fields - of which more in a moment.

Carry on and soon you will see the romantic ruins of the old village church that can be approached via a wrought iron gate. Take a moment to examine the gate: gradually the captivated forms of two lovers, birds, acorns and a deer will crystallize and may encourage you to explore this beautiful site. The current gate is a copy of an original that was presented by two residents to the parish in 1948. Shaw was present when the first was erected and

Ruins of the 12th century church demolished by Sir Lionel Lyde as it blocked his view.

gave a speech. He finished with the apposite words: "This is His House, this is His Gate and this is His Way."

The original church was constructed in the 12th century and the tower added in the 15th and 16th centuries. Sadly Sir Lionel Lyde, a former Lord of the Manor and a widely travelled man who had seen churches built in the modern style, demolished it in the 19th century. He used the bricks of the ruin to build the new parish church of St Lawrence in the Greek Revivalist style, which you have just seen across the fields. Thankfully, the Bishop of Lincoln intervened to prevent the old church's complete destruction, so we are left with these rather picturesque remains. Shaw was very attached to the remains and was often to be seen rambling through its arches and grounds.

On the right is a fine old Tudor Cottage and further on, just before The Brockett Arms, is a slightly dishevelled white house with an overgrown garden. The house used once to belong to the village postmistress Jisbella Lyth, whom Shaw immortalised in 1934, for she was the model of the heroine in the play "Village Wooing."

Shaw lived in London as well as in Ayot St Lawrence, but no matter where he was he always wrote to Jisbella for his stamps, using a post card in the process. She asked him once why he did so - even in Ayot for he could simply ask for them in the shop. He replied, "My dear woman, you shouldn't complain. You will be able to sell them (the post cards) for 2½d." "Tuppence ha'penny each indeed," she told him. "Why, I sell them for 10/6d. now." Furthermore the price that she was able to charge rose steadily until it reached three guineas. Jisbella was certainly an entrepreneur in contrast to the local taxi driver: when Shaw needed a car he also used a post card. The taxi driver threw all the post-cards - several hundred of them - on the fire. He was furious with himself when he learnt of the prices Jisbella was receiving.

The Brockett Arms is a traditionalist's idyllic pub with oak beams, an inglenook fireplace or two and lead windows. Shaw was a life long tee-totaller or at least he thought he was. He often drank in the pub - his preferred tipple was lemon juice - but the locals occasionally and mischievously spiked his drink with brandy.

Continue on for another 50 yards and turn left at the footpath sign for Codicote Bottom, then immediately right, through the kissing gate beyond the red-bricked Ayot-Lodge. Follow the path, keeping the fence to your left. Local legend has it that Henry VIII wooed Catherine Parr in the large manor house that you might just be able to see behind the well-trimmed yew hedge. As you stroll down the hill enjoy the glorious view of the countryside that opens up before you. At the end of the fence the path becomes a drive; keep going down, through the farmyard and turn left onto the road at the bottom and then right at the junction a few yards further on, signposted to Codicote.

Press on for 300 yards, over the hump back bridge that straddles the River Miriam, past Codicote Mill on the left, and then turn left onto the bridleway to Kimpton Mill. The path will soon veer to the right; it is bordered by oak and beech, holly and bramble, and beyond by tranquil water meadows.

Shaw's schedule included a daily six mile hike around Ayot St Lawrence, so you may well be treading in his footsteps. On a similar footing, the sister of Vincent Van Gogh lived in nearby Welwyn. The poverty stricken artist often visited her and made the trip from London on foot. As you amble along you might like to speculate whether any of the local views could have inspired his work.

Eventually you will come to a stile on the left. Climb over and cross the footbridge a few yards further on, then go over another stile. Continue across the meadow to the stile on the far side, over another footbridge (the brook below nurtures water cress) and you should finally emerge onto a road. Turn right, then after 30 yards, turn left onto the footpath opposite the Old Kempton Mill, signposted to Abbotshay.

Stay left of the trees as the path ascends next to the field. After 300 yards, the path will appear to widen and continue between two rows of hedges. Ignore this! Press on up the hill on the narrow path to the left of the hedges, but before you do so, pause for a moment. Look to the right and enjoy the stunning view of the river valley. You may see a church in the distance - the Church of St Peter and St Paul in the handsome town of Kimpton. Walk on for another 100 yards and the path will again lead between two hedges - this time wander in and climb to the top of the hill.

In front of you at the top is a fir hedge and the handsome buildings of Abbotshay Farm are on the right. Turn right and when the road curves to the left as a bridleway and cycle path, you will see a footpath to the right. Turn right onto the less inviting (but ultimately more interesting) footpath; follow it round to the left so that the tennis courts on the farm are behind you and the field is to your right. At the far end of the field, at the start of a diagonal line of trees, veer left and climb over the stile. Now aim for the roof of the building that emerges over the trees in the distance. The barbed wire fence on the left should drift diagonally away from you and a solitary scots pine tree should be to your right. As you cross the Manor House should come into view on the left. Go over the stile and straight on through the arched wrought iron gate that leads to the Parish Church of Ayot St Lawrence.

This is the new church built by Sir Lionel Lyde in 1788. Two colonnades lead left and right from the main building to two pavilions. Under one is the tomb of Sir Lionel and under the other, that of his wife. Apparently Sir Lionel did not enjoy a harmonious relationship with his wife and he vowed that since

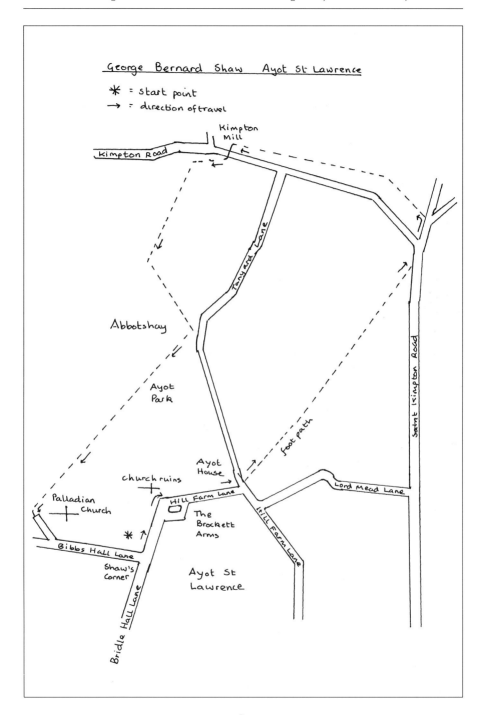

the Church had united them in life, it should make amends by separating them in death. Shaw, though a committed atheist, contributed generously to the upkeep of both churches, once donating £300 for roof repairs. He played the organ and occasionally played Bach or other favourite works here. If you wander around the churchyard, you might find the tombstone of Mary Ann South, born March 5th 1825, died February 13th 1895. The inscription that follows reads: in the midst of life we are in death, her time was short. Shaw related a story when asked why he had moved to the village that he saw this inscription when he first visited Ayot. "If they consider," he said, "the biblical three score years and ten a short life in Ayot, then Ayot is the place for me to grow old in!"

Follow the path across the churchyard then left and right until you come out onto the road. Turn left and Shaw's Corner can be found 100 yards further down the lane. Oddly, Shaw never shaved and he occasionally let his beard grow to a great length. As we conclude the walk you may wish to ponder, as did many of Shaw's fellow villagers, whether he slept with his beard inside or outside the sheets.

BIBLIOGRAPHY AND FURTHER READING:

Chappelow, Allen. Shaw the Chucker Out. London: George Allen & Unwin, 1969.
Chappelow, Allen. Shaw the Villager. London: George Allen & Unwin, 1971.
Shaw, G.B. Village Wooing. London: Constable & Co. Ltd., 1934.